Mastering the OGT

WRITING

Lesli J. Favor, Ph.D.

Amsco School Publications, Inc.
315 Hudson Street, New York, N.Y. 10013

for Steve, again!

Special thanks to Auditi Chakravarty, my wonderful, knowledgeable, and compassionate editor

Text and Cover Design: One Dot Inc.
Composition: Northeastern Graphic, Inc.
Art: Hadel Studio

When ordering this book, please specify:
Either **R 790 W** *or* **MASTERING THE OGT: WRITING.**

Please visit our Web site at: ***www.amscopub.com***

ISBN: 1-56765-112-7

Printed in the United States of America

1 2 3 4 5 6 7 8 9 10   08 07 06 05 04

About the Author

An educator for over a decade, Lesli J. Favor has written nine books for young adult readers and students. They include *Mastering the OGT: Reading*; *Mastering the OGT: Writing*; *The Iroquois Constitution*; *Italy: A Primary Source Cultural Guide*; and others. She earned her B.A. in English at the University of Texas at Arlington, then her M.A. and Ph.D. at the University of North Texas. She was assistant professor of English at Sul Ross State University–Rio Grande College. She lives in Dallas, Texas, with Steve (husband), Bouncer (dog), and Mr. Jack Legend (horse).

About the Consultants

Amy Dennis is a teacher for Columbus Public Schools in Columbus, Ohio. Formerly a Literacy Specialist and Title I Reading teacher, she currently serves as Testing Coordinator. Amy has degrees in Special Education: Hearing Impaired and in Elementary Education from Kent State University; Literacy and Learning from Ashland University; and a M.Ed. in Education Administration from Ohio State University.

Belinda Manard has served as an English Curriculum Specialist for Canton City Schools for the past eight years. Prior to that she taught English for nineteen years at McKinley Senior High in Canton, serving as Department Chair as well as the high school's test coordinator. She holds a B.S. in English, Communications, and Theater from Miami University of Ohio and a M.Ed. from the College of Mount St. Joseph. As a K–12 curriculum specialist for an urban district, Belinda develops and tests curriculum and assessments aligned with the new Ohio ELA Academic Content Standards, and provides staff development for teachers.

Peg Williams received her B.S. degree from Marshall University in Huntington, West Virginia. In 1978, she became Chairman of the English Department at Pickerington High School in Pickerington, Ohio. She continued her education by taking additional classes from Ohio State, Ohio University, and Concord College (West Virginia) and earned a Masters in Curriculum Development from Ashland University (Ohio). She has served on several educational committees for the Ohio Board of Education, such as the Senior English Ohio Scholastic Test and the Ohio Teacher Test.

Acknowledgments

Every effort has been made to obtain permission to use previously published materials. Any errors or omissions are unintentional.

OGT Writing rubrics and test blueprints, © 2004 Ohio Department of Education.

Page 29, prompt and sample response, © 2000 Ohio Department of Education.

Contents

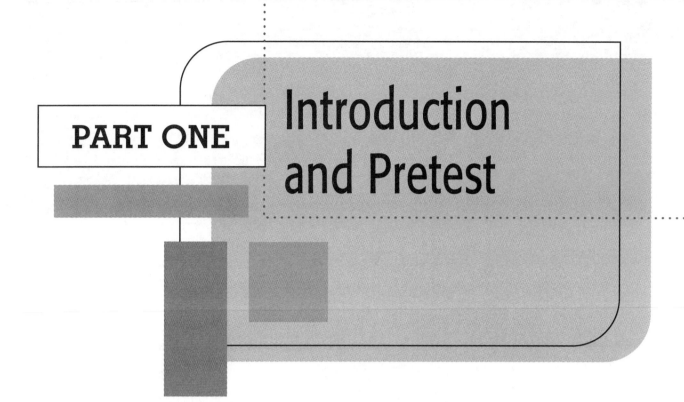

PART ONE

Introduction and Pretest

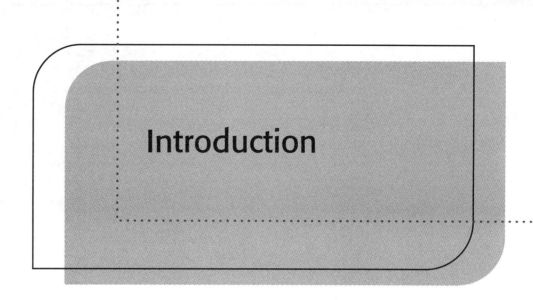

Introduction

To the Student

About the Ohio Graduation Test in Writing

The OGT Writing gives you the opportunity to demonstrate your skills and knowledge in three main areas:

1. Your ability to respond to writing topics, or prompts. Depending on the prompt, your writing may take the form of a persuasive piece, an expository passage, a letter, or a narrative. To produce your writing samples, you will be expected to follow the writing process, including prewriting, writing, revising, and editing.
2. Your knowledge of writing conventions—rules of spelling, punctuation, capitalization, and grammar—and your ability to apply them as part of the writing process.
3. Your ability to identify errors and revise them according to the conventions of writing.

The specific skills that will be tested on the OGT Writing are listed as *benchmarks*. The benchmarks are grouped into three sets:

- Benchmarks for the **writing process.** You'll find these benchmarks printed at the beginning of Lesson 1 in this book.
- Benchmarks for different **writing applications** (persuasive, informative, narrative). You'll find these benchmarks printed at the beginning of Lesson 1 in this book.
- Benchmarks for **writing conventions.** You'll find these benchmarks printed at the beginning of Lessons 2 and 3 in this book.

The test is made up of three parts. The first part asks you to respond to two different writing prompts. For this portion of the test, you will follow the writing process to develop and write each essay response. Of course, an essay you plan and write in a short amount of time is not expected to be as polished as one you write over a longer period of time, like many of your school assignments. However, each essay will show your abilities to plan, write, and revise a draft of an essay in one sitting.

Written responses are worth 9 points each and scored by two people. Therefore, the written portion of the OGT Writing is worth a total of 36 points. Lesson 1 in this book helps you prepare for this part of the test.

The second part of the OGT Writing asks you to answer multiple-choice questions. Each question is worth 1 point. Lessons 2 and 3 in this book help you prepare for this portion of the test.

In the third part of the test, you will explain, in your own words, how to revise an incorrect sentence according to the rules of grammar, spelling, punctuation, and capitalization. This constructed-response, or short-answer, item is worth two points.

In each lesson you will find several sections with these helpful features:

Look and Learn tells you about one or more skills or concepts to know for the test.

Try It Out gives you an opportunity to practice using one or more skills just taught. Usually, an example item is provided as a model to use in completing the rest of the items.

On Your Own is a mini–practice test for the OGT Writing. These questions cover the skills and concepts taught in the previous section of the lesson, such as 2.1 Spelling.

In addition, **OGT Practice** concludes Lessons 1, 2, and 3. This section lets you practice using all the skills taught in that lesson.

At the end of the book, you'll find two full-length practice tests. These are similar to what you'll experience on the actual OGT Writing and cover skills and concepts you learned in Lessons 1–3.

To the Teacher

The lessons in this book guide students in studying and practicing the skills tested by the **Ohio Graduation Test in Writing**.

The OGT Writing assesses students' skills relating to three standards within Ohio's *K–12 English Language Arts Academic Content Standards*.

- Writing Processes Standard
- Writing Applications Standard
- Writing Conventions Standard

All of the standards are assessed in the written portion of the test, in which students will respond to writing prompts. Each writing sample will be scored using a 6-point and a 3-point rubric.

The multiple-choice portion of the test will assess students' ability to edit and revise a passage. Students will be asked to choose the best way to revise part of a sentence, or recognize that the sentence needs no change. Each multiple-choice question is worth 1 point.

The 2-point constructed response item will check students' understanding of the rules that comprise the writing conventions. Students will be asked to revise an incorrectly written sentence and also to explain which rules govern the changes they choose to make.

Ohio Graduation Test in Writing

PART ONE: RESPONDING TO WRITING PROMPTS

Directions: Write a complete, edited response to each of the following two writing topics. You may start with either topic; divide your time as you think appropriate.

Use the blank pages for prewriting. Your prewriting is an important part of the writing process and should be completed. However, your prewriting will not be scored. The **drafts** you want **scored** should be written on the lined pages. These drafts need to be legible; they may be in printed or in cursive handwriting.

Revise and edit your writing. Erasing, crossing out, and other editing changes may be made right on the drafts themselves.

Go on to the next page.

TOPIC FOR WRITING #1

Recently your local newspaper published an article about the benefits of high school activities. The article claimed that music is not on the same level as other activities such as football, soccer, and basketball because music is not competitive, it's artistic. Do you agree or disagree with this statement? Write a letter to the editor of the newspaper, explaining your point of view. Use appropriate facts, opinions, and details to develop your letter.

Go on to the next page.

PREWRITING: Nothing on this page will be scored.

Go on to the next page.

Topic #1: Draft to be Scored

_____

_____

_____

_____

_____

_____

_____

_____

_____

_____

_____

_____

_____

_____

_____

_____

_____

_____

_____

_____

_____

_____

_____

Go on to the next page.

Go on to the next page.

TOPIC FOR WRITING #2

Write a story about a narrow escape from trouble. The events may be real or imagined. Tell what the trouble was, who (or what creature) escaped it, and how. Develop your story with details.

Go on to the next page.

PREWRITING: Nothing on this page will be scored.

Go on to the next page.

Topic #2: Draft to be Scored

_____

_____

_____

_____

_____

_____

_____

_____

_____

_____

_____

_____

_____

_____

_____

_____

_____

_____

_____

_____

_____

Go on to the next page.

Go on to the next page.

PART TWO: RESPONDING TO MULTIPLE-CHOICE QUESTIONS

Instructions: Certain words and phrases in the following passage are underlined and numbered. In the right-hand column, you will find alternatives for each underlined part. Choose the alternative showing the best way to revise and improve the selection. If the original version is best, choose NO CHANGE.

The Value of a Dollar

Dad said that in his day, everyone talked about the value of a dollar. Today, a dollar <u>doesnt</u> go
1
very far. When a fast-food lunch costs five dollars,

      1. **A.** NO CHANGE
           B. does'not
           C. doesn't
           D. does'nt

<u>a shirt in the mall thirty dollars,</u> and basketball
2
sneakers cost seventy-five dollars, I ask you: What does

one dollar buy anymore?

      2. **A.** NO CHANGE
           B. a shirt in the mall costs thirty dollars
           C. a shirt in the mall costing thirty dollars
           D. a shirt thirty dollars in the mall

I happen to have a great group of friends. Being

<u>bored, we</u> decided to test the value of a dollar.
3
However, we didn't want simply to spend the dollar but

      3. **A.** NO CHANGE
           B. bored we
           C. bored. We
           D. bored,

<u>making money from it.</u> How did we do that?
4

      4. **A.** NO CHANGE
           B. to make money from it
           C. to have made money from it
           D. make money from it

First, we each <u>through</u> one dollar into a hat. We took
5
our hat of dollars to a local discount store and bought

      5. **A.** NO CHANGE
           B. thorough
           C. thru
           D. threw

Go on to the next page.

bulk wrapped candy. Before you laugh too hard at us,

read on. We took the candy to <u>school</u> and sold it, piece
6

by piece, for a profit. When we put all the money into

the hat once again, our dollars had doubled.

From there we took on a bigger <u>project</u> a car wash
7

every day for a week. Each day, we set it up at a

different house or location where we had permission.

When we put our money into the hat at the end of the

<u>week. It had</u> more than doubled!
8

Thrilled, the value of a dollar was becoming apparent.
9

We set about making plans <u>keep</u> our money working for
10

us. After all, we have expenses: fast-food lunches, shirts,

shoes—and even bigger stuff, like college.

_____ **6. A.** NO CHANGE
     B. School
     C. skool
     D. scool

_____ **7. A.** NO CHANGE
     B. project:
     C. project;
     D. project.

_____ **8. A.** NO CHANGE
     B. week, It had
     C. week, it had
     D. week it had

_____ **9. A.** NO CHANGE
     B. Thrilled that
     C. Thrilled, we
        thought
     D. Thrilled about

_____ **10. A.** NO CHANGE
     B. for keep
     C. keeping
     D. to keep

Go on to the next page.

PART THREE: RESPONDING TO A SHORT-ANSWER QUESTION

Instructions: Use the checklist to answer the following question.

Writer's Checklist

Good writing includes the following:

✓ Standard English
✓ Noun/verb agreement
✓ Correct use of pronouns
✓ Parallel structure
✓ Proper punctuation

Every year, my father and me complete a project that allows us to spend time together, giving back to the community, and had fun with each other.

You have been asked by a fellow student to peer edit the above sentence. Using the checklist, give the writer feedback by identifying the two rules that apply to the errors in the sentence. Then rewrite the sentence correctly.

_____

_____

_____

_____

_____

_____

_____

_____

STOP

Pretest Checklist

Written Response Section

Written responses on the OGT are scored using criteria called *rubrics*. A rubric describes the requirements a response must meet in order to earn a specific score. Each response is scored with two rubrics: a six-point holistic rubric and a three-point conventions rubric. Item-specific rubrics for the two prompts are shown below, followed by the three-point conventions rubric. With your teacher's help, use these criteria to evaluate your written responses.

6-point Item-Specific Rubric for Topic #1

Points	Scoring Criteria
6	This is a superior piece of writing. The response is clearly focused on the question of whether music is on the same level as other activities. The response is clearly written as a letter to the editor and a strong sense of audience and purpose is maintained throughout. It has a clear beginning, middle, and end. The writer's ideas are clearly stated and richly developed, and they flow in a unified, cohesive sequence. Ample compelling details support the writer's main idea, and information is clearly and logically organized. The sentence structure shows sophistication and variety, and the style is engaging. Vocabulary and diction is precise and effective.
5	This is an excellent piece of writing. The response focuses on the question of whether music is on the same level as other activities and is written as a letter to the editor. It shows a sense of audience and purpose throughout. The response is clearly organized with a beginning, middle, and end. The writer's ideas and opinions are clear and well supported and structured in a coherent, unified manner. Sentence structure is varied and the writer's style is often engaging. Vocabulary and diction are varied and effective.
4	This is an effective piece of writing. The response is generally related to the question of whether music is on the same level as other activities and shows a general sense of purpose. It may not be addressed to the editor but it shows an awareness of audience. Details are generally relevant, although some information may go off topic. Paragraph development may be inconsistent, while ideas are generally unified, cohesive, and well organized, with only occasional lapses. Sentence structure and vocabulary may be varied and style is effective.
3	This is an adequate piece of writing. The response is generally relevant to the question of whether music is on the same level as other activities, and it shows a general awareness of audience and purpose, though there are inconsistencies throughout. Details and examples are included, but they may be

repetitive, uneven, or inappropriate. The organization plan is acceptable, and the sequence and structure of ideas is somewhat unified and coherent. Varied sentence structure is occasionally evidenced, and word choice and style are appropriate.

2   This is a marginal piece of writing. While there is an attempt to address the question of whether music is on the same level as other activities, the response shows an inconsistent awareness of audience and purpose. Ideas and details are inadequate and are often repetitive, unevenly developed, or inappropriate. The organization plan is noticeably lacking, as are unity and cohesion of ideas. There are lapses in sentence structure throughout, and word choice and style are often unclear.

1   This is an inadequate piece of writing. The response is weakly connected to the topic and shows no awareness of audience or purpose. There is little or no development of ideas and the writer's thoughts are unclear or undeveloped. There is little or no organizational structure, and there are severe lapses in sentence structure, appropriate word choice, and readable style.

0   This response cannot be scored for it is completely off-topic, illegible, in a language other than English, or blank.

6-point Item-Specific Rubric for Topic #2

Points   **Scoring Criteria**

6   This is a superior piece of writing. The response clearly addresses the prompt and presents a focused narrative about a narrow escape from trouble. A consistent sense of audience is maintained throughout the response. The narrative tells what the trouble is, who (or what creature) escapes it, and how. The plot has a strong beginning, middle, and end, with conflict, rising tension, a climax, and a resolution. The story is richly developed with ample details that are logical and relevant to the story. Sentence structure is varied and vocabulary and style are highly engaging.

5   This is an excellent piece of writing. The response addresses the prompt and presents a narrative about a narrow escape from trouble. A sense of audience is evident throughout. The narrative tells what the trouble is, who (or what) escapes it, and how. The plot has a beginning, middle, and end, with some elements of conflict, tension, climax, and resolution. The story is developed with many details that are clearly organized. Sentence structure shows variety and vocabulary and style are engaging.

4   This is an effective piece of writing. The response generally develops a narrative that addresses the prompt. The response shows some elements of narrative, such as setting, character, and conflict. Story elements may not show precise plot organization of conflict—rising tension—climax—resolution. Events and dialogue are generally relevant to the prompt, though details may be inconsistent or diverge from the focus on a narrow escape from trouble. Sentence structure, vocabulary, and style are effective.

3 This is an adequate piece of writing. The response is related to the prompt, but the narrative may include inconsistencies. Elements of narrative, such as setting, character, and plot, are evidenced, but may be unclear or poorly developed. Plot elements of rising tension, climax, and resolution are poorly executed or presented out of order. Sentence structure is adequate, and style and word choice are adequate.

2 This is a marginal piece of writing. The response is loosely related to the prompt, but the narrative is inconsistent and poorly developed. Important elements, such as setting, character, and plot, are unclear or inappropriate. Plot elements may not exist. There are lapses in sentence structure and word choice, and style is limited.

1 This is an inadequate piece of writing. The response barely addresses the topic and a sense of audience is absent. Story elements may be missing or unclear, and any details or events are undeveloped. There are serious lapses in sentence structure, word choice is inappropriate, and the style is unclear.

0 This response cannot be scored for it is completely off-topic, illegible, in a language other than English, or blank.

3-point Conventions Rubric for Topics #1 and #2

Points	Scoring Criteria
3	The response is free from any errors that impair the reader's understanding and comprehension. Few errors, if any, are present in capitalization, punctuation, and spelling. The writing displays a consistent understanding of grammatical conventions.
2	Occasional errors may impair a reader's understanding of the written response. Some capitalization, punctuation, and spelling errors are present. The writing displays some understanding of grammatical conventions.
1	Errors are frequent and impair a reader's understanding of the written response. Numerous errors in capitalization, punctuation, and spelling are present. The writing displays a minimal understanding of grammatical conventions.

OR

The length and complexity of the response is insufficient to demonstrate that the writer has control over standard English conventions

0 The response cannot be scored because it is off-task, completely illegible, in a language other than English, or blank.

Multiple-Choice Section

The following checklist will help you evaluate your performance on the multiple-choice section of the Pretest. Look at column 1 for each correct answer, and mark the box in column 2 for each answer you missed. Each question is worth 1 point.

Now take a moment to glance at column 2. The questions you answered correctly show your strengths, and the questions you missed show the areas in which you need more work. Column 3 shows which sections of this book will help you review the skills you need to master the questions you missed. In column 4, page numbers tell you where to turn in this book for each section.

Answer	Check if Missed	Review This Lesson	Page
1. C	☐	2.2 Punctuation	73
2. B	☐	3.5 Parallel Structure	141
3. A	☐	3.3 Phrases 3.4 Modifiers	114 126
4. B	☐	3.3 Phrases 3.5 Parallel Structure	114 141
5. D	☐	2.1 Spelling	64
6. A	☐	2.1 Spelling 2.3 Capitalization	64 86
7. B	☐	2.2 Punctuation	73
8. C	☐	2.2 Punctuation 2.3 Capitalization 3.2 Clauses: Main and Subordinate	73 90 107
9. C	☐	3.4 Modifiers	126
10. D	☐	3.3 Phrases	114

Short Answer Section

The short-answer question is worth two points. In order to earn full credit, you must correctly identify two errors in the sentence and write the sentence correctly. If you complete only a portion of this task correctly, you will earn one point. There may be more than one correct way to revise the sentence, but following is an example of a full-score response:

> Two errors appear in this sentence. First, the writer incorrectly uses the objective pronoun "me" when the subject form should be used. There is also a problem with parallel structure because

"giving" and "had" should appear in the same verb tense as "spend." The sentence could be correctly rewritten as follows:

> Every year, my father and I complete a project that allows us to spend time together, to give back to the community, and to have fun with each other.

With your teacher's help and the above example, you can check how many points your response would earn.

PART TWO

Mastering the OGT Writing

Writing Processes Benchmarks

A. Formulate writing ideas and identify a topic appropriate to the purpose and audience.

B. Determine the usefulness of organizers and apply appropriate pre-writing tasks.

C. Use revision strategies to improve the style, variety of sentence structure, clarity of the controlling idea, logic, effectiveness of word choice and transitions between paragraphs, passages or ideas.

D. Edit to improve sentence fluency, grammar and usage.

E. Apply tools to judge the quality of writing.

F. Prepare writing for publication that is legible, follows an appropriate format and uses techniques such as electronic resources and graphics.

Writing Applications Benchmarks

A. Compose narratives that establish a specific setting, plot and a consistent point of view, and develop characters by using sensory details and concrete language.

B. Write responses to literature that extend beyond the summary and support references to the text, other works, other authors or to personal knowledge.

C. Produce letters (e.g., business, letters to the editor, job applications) that follow the conventional style appropriate to the text and that include appropriate details and exclude extraneous details and inconsistencies.

D. Use documented textual evidence to justify interpretations of literature or to support a research topic.

E. Write a persuasive piece that states a clear position, includes relevant information and offers compelling evidence in the form of facts and details.

Have you written an e-mail message or letter recently? Think about to whom you wrote. What did you want to tell the person? Did you write a quick, informal note, or did you write a longer, carefully worded message?

The form of the message and the words you used depended on *whom* you were writing to and *why* you wrote. As most people do with all kinds of writing, you naturally tailored your e-mail message to fit your *audience* and *purpose*.

Whether you are writing e-mail messages, letters, or essays, you need to think about three key aspects of writing:

- the purpose of writing
- the process of writing
- the mechanics of writing (spelling, punctuation, capitalization, grammar)

The Ohio Graduation Test in Writing will give you an opportunity to demonstrate your skills in these areas. On the test, you'll be asked to respond to two different writing topics, or prompts. Each prompt will require an essay that fits in one of three main categories.

- **Expository** writing *explains* a subject or topic to readers, or *informs* readers about a topic. Expository writing makes the subject clear by including sufficient details and by presenting information logically. The expository text may use persuasive techniques, description, or narration as needed to further clarify the information.

- **Persuasive** writing gives a clear *opinion or point of view* on a topic or subject, and it offers details and evidence to support the viewpoint. Its main purpose is to convince readers to take on a particular belief or viewpoint or to take a particular action.

- **Narrative** writing tells a *story or account* of real or imaginary events. A narrative establishes a setting and characters, relates a plot, and uses a consistent point of view. Characters and actions are developed with sensory details and concrete language.

The OGT Writing will ask you to write two passages, each in response to a different prompt or topic. You may be asked, for example, to write a persuasive essay supporting or opposing your school's dress code. Or you may be asked to write a narrative about a time you made a new friend.

Your two written responses are equally important and are worth 6 points each. You will need to plan your time so that you are able to complete each response fully. You'll want to follow the steps of the writing process as you write each draft—prewriting, writing, and revising.

Whatever the writing topic, you will be given space on the test for prewriting—a chance to develop ideas in a space that will NOT be scored. You will also be given lined pages on which to write your final draft, which will be scored. You will revise and edit your final draft right there on the copy to be scored.

Lesson 1 will help you prepare for the OGT Writing in these important ways:

- You'll learn the scoring guidelines for the OGT Writing.

- You'll review the basic steps in a writing process.

- You'll practice responding to expository, persuasive, and narrative writing topics.

Look ahead to Lesson 2 as well, where you will learn the writing conventions that you need to know for scoring well on your writing prompts. In addition, look for other opportunities to improve your writing skills. For instance, study the types of writing you encounter in your classes, read books and newspapers and Web sites, and use correct grammar and spelling no matter what you write. Just as a musician develops an ear for music by repeated exposure to good music, you can develop an instinct for writing by exposing yourself to many different kinds of good writing.

Look & Learn

Think back to the last time you entered a competition. What did you think about ahead of the event? If you're like most people, you wanted to know what to expect in the competition and how your performance would be evaluated. Knowing the answers to these questions helps you prepare and do your best.

The written portion of the OGT Writing is no different. You want to know what to expect on the test, and you want to know what criteria will be used to score your work.

You can expect to see two writing prompts on the test. Depending on the prompt, you will respond by writing an essay, a letter, or other piece of writing. For each writing topic, you'll be given blank pages for brainstorming, outlining, and other prewriting activities. You'll also be given lined pages on which to write your draft to be scored. Once you've written the draft, you will revise and edit it by erasing, crossing out, and rewriting right there on the copy to be scored.

Written responses will be graded by specially trained readers. To decide how many points a response has earned, readers will use an established set of rules called a *rubric*. In this way, the responses of students all across Ohio are scored using the exact same criteria.

Two rubrics are used to score the OGT essays, one worth six points, the other worth three points. This means a full score is 9 points, and the lowest possible score is a 0. A full-score response meets all the criteria described in both of the following rubrics. In the column to the right of the rubrics, key elements are explained in more detail.

In the Spotlight

Holistic rubric for full-score response

The response directly addresses the prompt, the purpose is clearly understood, and a sense of audience is consistently maintained throughout. It is richly developed with compelling ideas, examples, and details. These ideas are unified and flow in a smooth, coherent sequence as part of a clear and precise organizational plan that actively engages the reader.

Explanation

Focus: All ideas and details logically support a clear central idea.
Audience: The paper is tailored to the appropriate kind of reader.
Content: The topic is well developed with specific ideas and information.
Structure: The paper is organized so that ideas flow smoothly from one to the next.

The response consistently demonstrates a variety in sentence structures. Vocabulary is broad, precise, and carefully chosen to address the purpose and audience. Word choice is varied and effective, and style is engaging.

Conventions rubric for full-score response

The response is free from errors that impair a reader's understanding and comprehension. Few errors, if any, are present in capitalization, punctuation, and spelling. The writing displays a consistent understanding of grammatical conventions.

Think of the scoring process as measuring different levels of strength in students' papers. Have you ever seen one of those "tests of strength" at a carnival or amusement park? There is a tall column with a bell at the top, and at the bottom is a target for you to hit with a giant hammer. A really strong whack on the target causes a marker to rocket up the tower and ring the bell. Less forceful hits send the marker up only partway, and a really weak hit hardly moves the marker at all.

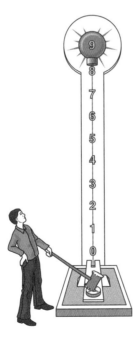

On the OGT Writing, a strong paper meeting the scoring standards fully will rocket to the top and earn a 9. A paper with weakness in one or two areas will shoot up to a 7. A paper with a few more weaknesses rises to a 5. You get the idea. A paper that is completely off-topic, is completely illegible, is in a language other than English, or is blank (no response) receives a 0.

The following box contains a writing prompt like the ones you'll see on the OGT. This particular prompt asks for a persuasive response in the form of a letter to the school principal.

> Your principal is considering a ban on activities such as field trips, assemblies, and pep rallies because they interfere with classroom learning. Consider whether you are for or against the ban. Then write a letter to your principal convincing him or her to see your point of view. Be specific in developing your argument.

A full-score response to this prompt would meet all the requirements listed in the two scoring rubrics. Take a moment to re-read the rubrics and the explanations (they're on pages 27–28).

Now take a look at the sample student response below. This is an actual student paper, written in response to the writing prompt you just read. It earned a full score of 9. As you read, watch for ways the response meets the scoring criteria regarding *focus, content, structure, purpose, audience,* and *writing conventions.*

Dear Principal,

I was surprised and disappointed when I learned that you are planning to ban "noneducational" activities. As a member of Student Council and Class President, I speak for the entire student body in saying that banning these activities would be anything but productive.

The lessons taught in our classrooms only prepare us for a fraction of what we will encounter in the real world. Holding assemblies every month or so gives us the opportunity to experience various choices and options, such as college and career choices and opportunities within our own school. Without these, students are limited as to what challenges we may tackle in the near future. Assemblies help to enlighten us and open our minds, and doing away with them could limit our productivity in society.

Also, banning field trips would be a terrible decision to make. We can only learn so much about science in the science lab, and a day at the science center is worth a month in the classroom. Taking field trips allows us to go out and get hands-on experience concerning subject matter that we may have not have understood or enjoyed otherwise. Likewise, trips to various colleges and jobsites over the course of a year can help us to better decide in what direction we would like to go with our lives. Classroom learning can be helpful, but not taking advantage of available knowledge, information, and experiences would be a step in the wrong direction.

Furthermore, banning pep rallies would be more harmful than helpful to students. Pep rallies give us a chance to join together and show a type of companionship in schools. They also encourage participation in a very fun way and give kids something to look forward to. Without activities encouraging participation and companionship, schools would not be fully doing their jobs.

Schools are not just buildings to which children are sent to learn to read and do math anymore. The objective of schools is to show students their options, to give them real-life experience, and to teach them as much as possible. Reducing or banning outside-of-the-classroom activities would defeat the purpose of schools and would keep students from becoming well-rounded. As the world around us takes giant steps forward each day, schools must keep up with them to produce compitent people for the workplace. Limiting student experience would harm our chances to be successful in the future and be a terrible mistake to be made.

Thank you for taking the time to read my letter, and I hope that you will consider my opinion when making a decision.

Sincerely Yours,

Evaluate a Student Response

Answer the following questions about the sample student response. The questions are grouped according to the key criteria described in the scoring rubric.

Focus

1. Upon what central idea/topic did the writer focus in the sample response?

2. Specifically, what is the writer's point of view on this topic?

_____

Content
   3. What four main ideas does the writer discuss in the body of the paper?

_____

_____

Structure
   4. List at least three transitional words and phrases the writer uses to show the relationships between ideas.

_____

   5. How does the writer give the letter a sense of closure?

_____

Purpose
   6. What is the writer's purpose in writing the letter? Identify any technique(s) the writer uses to achieve this purpose and evaluate their effectiveness.

_____

_____

   7. List at least three well-chosen words or phrases the writer uses to help express his or her ideas and achieve his or her purpose.

_____

Audience
   8. Who is the audience (intended reader) of the letter? Is this the same audience that the writing prompt requires the writer to address?

_____

Writing Conventions
   9. There is only one misspelled word in the paper. Can you find it? Write it as the student misspelled it; then write the correct spelling beside it.

_____

10. The writer uses awkward or incorrect phrasing only a couple of times in the paper. Write one example of awkward or incorrect usage here.

As you prepare to take the written portion of the OGT Writing, remember these tips:

- The key to doing well on the written response section is *being able to express yourself clearly in writing.*

- To develop your ability to express yourself in writing, *take advantage of any opportunity you have to practice writing.* For example, keep a daily journal about your personal experiences or school-related events. Revise entries to make them more clear and specific. For example, use a thesaurus or dictionary to expand your vocabulary, inserting well-chosen words in place of less specific words. Practice choosing a focus for an entry and staying on-topic. Cross out sentences and paragraphs that go off-topic, and add relevant information when appropriate.

- To develop a sense of how to express yourself in writing, *read good writing.* You'll get ideas for how to write that important first sentence, how to structure sentences, how to organize the paragraphs within an essay, how to use new words, and so on.

- Keep in mind that *you will not necessarily feel enthusiastic about the writing topics* given to you on the test. This doesn't mean that you won't be able to write a strong response. Approach each writing opportunity as a professional, and you'll get the job done because you have prepared, not because you worked off emotion.

- *Practice writing neatly and clearly.* Remember, the scoring officials can give you credit only for what they can read.

- Finally, become familiar with the *key elements of a full-score response* remembering that one element, **conventions**, is worth three points:

Content	Audience	Focus
Purpose	Structure	Writing Conventions

These six elements form the focus of the two scoring rubrics used to grade your responses. Using the rubric as a checklist, official graders will look for these elements in your work.

Sections 1.2 and 1.3 of Lesson 1 explain more about these key elements. Keep reading!

Look & Learn

In Greek mythology, goddesses called Muses provided inspiration to artists, musicians, and writers. Today, you may hear a writer say that she has "lost her muse" and therefore cannot write. Other writers simply say that they need to feel inspired to write. Or have you ever put off writing a paper until you "felt like writing"?

We have all resorted to these stalling techniques. Writing is hard mental work, and we'll look for any way to put it off or make it easier.

This approach to writing breaks down, however, when you put yourself in a testing environment. When a test booklet is placed before you, what can you do if you feel like you've "lost your muse"?

This dilemma is the reason why writers rely on the writing process. By using a process of identifying a topic, generating ideas, organizing information, writing a draft, and revising the draft, you can produce a writing sample whether or not you feel inspired. True, you may feel better about a piece you write when you were in the mood to write. But on a test, the most important thing is to get the job done, and this requires confidence rather than inspiration.

In the Spotlight

The Writing Process

You may be familiar with the main steps of the writing process.

Prewriting—generating ideas, planning content, organizing information

Writing—using the prewriting efforts to guide you in writing a draft that is focused, clear, and well organized

Revising—making changes to strengthen the draft, such as crossing out information that is off-topic or adding an important point of information. This step also includes **editing**—proofreading and correcting errors in grammar and spelling.

Publishing—submitting the writing to one or more readers

As you work through this lesson and learn more about the writing process, you'll also learn about different writing forms and purposes. Specifically, this section uses expository and persuasive writing to help demonstrate the writing process. The next section, 1.3—

Narrative Writing, specifically addresses the writing process and narratives.

1: Prewriting

Whether you are going for a hike, baking a casserole, building a doghouse, or creating a football strategy, you must first do one thing: Make a plan. The same is true in writing. To produce a clear, focused, well-developed essay, you need to plan the writing first, then write the draft.

Decoding the Writing Prompt

Before you can plan the content of your paper, you need to know what you're being asked to write about. To do so, you must decode the writing prompt—read it and understand exactly what it is asking for. On the OGT Writing, plan to read each writing prompt at least three times, looking for specific information each time.

- **First:** Read the entire prompt to get an overall understanding of what it is about. What is the central topic of the prompt? The topic tells you what kind of **content** your paper should have.

- **Second:** Read the prompt again more slowly, looking for signal words that tell you the **purpose** of your paper. The purpose will be one of the following:

    Inform—Explain facts, ideas, or other information. This type of writing is also called expository writing.

    Persuade—Convince the reader to take on a belief or opinion, or to take a specific action.

    Narrate—Tell a sequence of events or experiences in narrative form.

- **Third:** Read the prompt again, looking for specific pieces of information your paper must include. For instance, does the prompt require you to state a clear opinion on a topic? Does it identify who the **audience** of your paper should be? Does it tell you what **form** your essay should take, such as a letter or simple essay?

In the chart that follows is an example of a writing prompt that asks you to write a paper to **inform**. In the right column, you'll see how you can study the prompt to determine exactly what it is asking for.

WRITING TOPIC	**YOU MAY THINK . . .**
Your town's Chamber of Commerce is creating a Web site called "About Our Town" that will inform current and new residents of the town's many fine attributes. For the Web site, write an essay on your school, telling what the school offers students your age. Include specific details and examples to make your ideas clear.	The first sentence gives me context for my essay—an informative Web site. From this, I can conclude that I should write an essay to <u>inform</u>. The word " telling" also signals that I should <u>inform</u> about the topic. The last sentence reminds me to use details and examples to support my ideas.

Now read the following example of a prompt asking you to write a paper to **persuade**. To the right of the prompt is an example of how you can read the prompt to determine exactly what it asks of you.

WRITING TOPIC	**YOU MAY THINK . . .**
The president of the Student Council is deciding whether to propose a recycling program for your school, but he or she is unsure if there is enough student support. Do you think there should or should not be a recycling program? Write a letter to the Student Council president persuading him or her to see your point of view. Be specific in developing your argument.	The first sentence tells me that someone is trying to make a decision. This is a clue that I will be writing to <u>persuade</u> him or her about what to decide. The next sentence asks me what I think, so I have to express an <u>opinion</u>. The last sentence tells me my answer should take the form of a <u>letter</u>; words like "persuading" and "point of view" indicate that a persuasive essay is required. "Be specific" means I should state my opinion clearly and back it up with particular reasons.

Decode a Writing Prompt

Practice reading a prompt to determine exactly what it asks for. Read the prompt below; then answer the questions that follow it.

> Your principal is trying to decide whether or not the cheerleading program is necessary. The principal is considering canceling the cheerleading squad and suggesting that the cheerleaders sign up for sports instead. Do you think the cheerleading program is necessary at your school? Write a letter to the principal persuading him or her to see your point of view. Be specific in developing your argument.

1. What **topic** does the writing prompt ask you to write about?

_____

2. What is the **purpose** of your paper?

_____

3. Who is the **audience** for this paper?

_____

4. In what **form** should your response be written?

_____

Think It Through

1. In this prompt, the topic is stated in the first sentence. It is the question of "whether or not the cheerleading program is necessary." The second sentence in the prompt gives additional information and ideas in support of the topic.

2. The third sentence in the prompt asks you for an opinion about the topic. This is a clue that you should write a persuasive paper. Your goal is to convince readers to agree with your opinion. Another clue that the paper should be persuasive is the word _persuading_ in the fourth sentence.

3. The fourth sentence in the prompt tells you who your audience is— the principal. Your goal in writing the paper is to persuade the principal to agree with your opinion about cheerleaders.

4. The fourth sentence in the prompt also tells you the form of your essay—a letter to the principal.

As you can see, by carefully reading (and re-reading!) the writing prompt, you identify four things: your paper's topic, purpose, audience, and form. Thinking about these elements is an important part of the prewriting stage of a typical writing process.

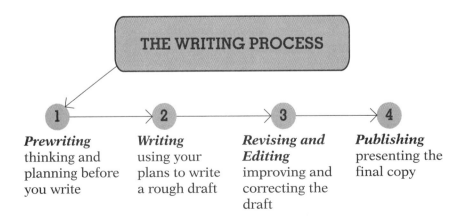

1	**2**	**3**	**4**
Prewriting thinking and planning before you write	_Writing_ using your plans to write a rough draft	_Revising and Editing_ improving and correcting the draft	_Publishing_ presenting the final copy

As the preceding diagram shows, another key part of the prewriting stage is planning. Your goals during this stage are to generate ideas about the topic and to think about how you can organize them to form a structured, focused essay. Here are a few techniques many writers find useful at this stage.

Prewriting Techniques

- **Freewriting** is a great idea generator. Write your topic at the top of the page. Below that, write down as many ideas about the topic as possible. Keep writing without stopping for about five minutes. Your goal is to let ideas flow freely out of your mind and onto the page. Let your ideas come out in any form—words, phrases, or sentences—but don't stop to correct or judge the writing. If you get stuck, write the same word or idea repeatedly until something new occurs to you. When you're done, you can underline the strongest or most promising ideas to use in your essay. Use this technique to "kick-start" your brain any time you get stuck during your writing process.

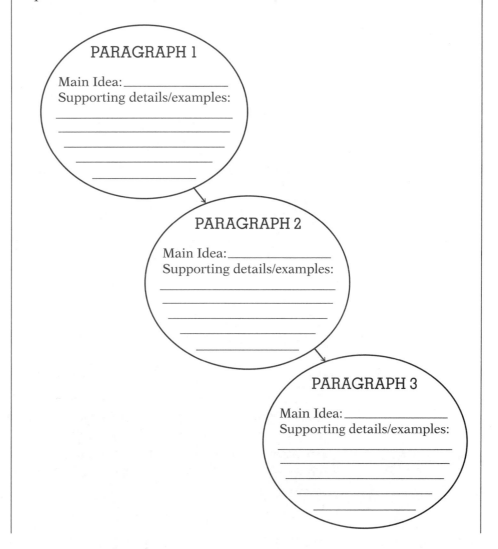

PARAGRAPH 1

Main Idea:_____
Supporting details/examples:

_____
_____
_____
_____
_____

PARAGRAPH 2

Main Idea:_____
Supporting details/examples:

_____
_____
_____
_____
_____

PARAGRAPH 3

Main Idea:_____
Supporting details/examples:

_____
_____
_____
_____
_____

- A **Cluster Diagram** or **Planning Web** can help you generate ideas, organize them, or both. Draw a circle in the center of your paper and write your topic inside it. Around the outside of the circle, draw more circles and connect them to the central one with lines. Inside each outer circle, write an idea or detail that connects to the main topic. To add more ideas and details, create new circles to link to existing circles. In the end, the placement and pattern of circles is up to you. An example is shown on the facing page, and another one is included in the discussion about the expository writing prompt.
- **Outline** Write your topic at the top of your page. Underneath, use roman numerals to list the main ideas about the topic, leaving a few blank lines between each numeral. Under each main idea, use capital letters to list supporting details. For a less formal outline, use dashes or bullets instead of numerals and letters.

FORMAL OUTLINE

I. Idea about topic
    A. Supporting detail/example
        1. related detail
        2. related detail
    B. Supporting detail/example

INFORMAL OUTLINE

1. Idea about topic
    • Supporting detail/example
      –related detail
      –related detail
    • Supporting detail/example

- **Five Ws and How** Ask questions about your topic to prompt yourself to provide answers and details. Along the left margin of your page, write the following questions: Who? What? When? Where? Why? How? Between each one, leave space to write. Use each word to generate questions about your topic, and then answer the questions to generate details and information.

The sample expository writing topic is printed again below. Read it again, and then look at the idea organizers that follow it.

Your town's Chamber of Commerce is creating a Web site called "About Our Town" that will inform current and new residents of the town's many fine attributes. For the Web site, write an essay on your school, telling what the school offers students your age. Include specific details and examples to make your ideas clear.

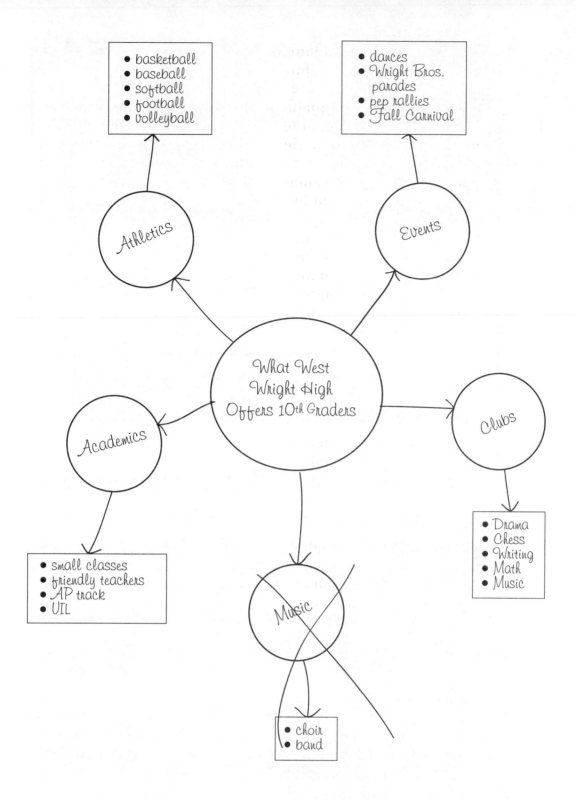

- basketball
- baseball
- softball
- football
- volleyball

- dances
- Wright Bros. parades
- pep rallies
- Fall Carnival

Athletics

Events

What West Wright High Offers 10th Graders

Academics

Clubs

- small classes
- friendly teachers
- AP track
- UIL

- Drama
- Chess
- Writing
- Math
- Music

Music

- choir
- band

In the cluster diagram, notice that the writer crossed out "music" as a main topic and listed it instead as a supporting detail under "clubs." Because a cluster diagram lets you visualize your ideas, revising it can be a great way to reorganize your thoughts before you start writing.

TOPIC: What West Wright High Offers 10th Graders

1. Academics   3. Clubs

   • Small classes   • Drama

   • Friendly teachers   • Chess

   • Advanced Placement   • Writing

   (AP) track   • Math

   • University Interscholastic League   • Music

2. Athletics   4. Events

   • Basketball   • Dances

   • Baseball   • Yearly Wright Brothers Parade

   • Softball   • Pep rallies

   • Football   • Fall Carnival

   • Volleyball

In this informal outline, the writer has organized information into four sections. Each section will form part of the body of the draft. Notice that in this outline, the writer has not listed ideas for the introduction or the conclusion. As a result, the writer may have difficulty writing clear, focused paragraphs for these important parts of the essay.

2: Writing

By now you have determined what the writing prompt asks for (the topic, audience, and purpose), and you have generated ideas and details. Now you are ready to write your essay. No two papers are exactly alike, even if they are written on the same topic. But all papers should share a few basic structural elements.

Structure of an Informative or Persuasive Paper

INTRODUCTION
introduces the topic and gives the thesis statement

BODY
develops, supports, and/or proves the main idea or thesis

CONCLUSION
sums up the most important ideas and gives closure to the paper

---

The structure of your paper gives organization and shape to the content. Let's look more closely at what kinds of content to put into the three main sections of your paper.

Introduction

The introduction, usually the first paragraph of your paper, has three main purposes: (1) to identify the paper's topic; (2) to state the paper's thesis; and (3) to hook your reader's interest.

- The *topic* is the main idea of the paper. On the OGT Writing, a writing prompt will give you a topic for your paper.

- The *thesis* is your viewpoint on the topic. Think of the topic as a noun, and the thesis as a noun plus a verb.

  noun: your <u>school</u> *(topic)*

  noun + verb: <u>West Wright High</u> <u>enriches</u> students' lives.
                        (thesis)

  Of course, you can add details to this basic format to make the thesis even more specific. For example, *West Wright High enriches students' lives through academics, sports, clubs, and special events.*

- The **hook** that snags your reader's interest will vary, depending on your topic and purpose. On the OGT, an interesting fact or opinion that helps introduce your topic works well. Famous quotations, lines from well-known poems or songs, or rhetorical questions are other good hooks that can get a reader's attention.

Body

Once you have introduced your reader to the topic and thesis of the paper, it's time to develop the thesis. How you develop the thesis depends on your writing purpose. A persuasive paper offers opinions along with information to support those opinions. An informative paper offers facts, details, and descriptions. These paragraphs, which follow the introduction and come before the conclusion, are the body of your paper.

- A *body paragraph* is made up of a group of related sentences. Each paragraph focuses on one idea that supports your thesis. Within each paragraph, each detail supports, develops, or clarifies the paragraph's main idea.

- A *topic sentence* states the main idea of a paragraph. Usually the topic sentence comes first in the paragraph, or close to the beginning. Sometimes it occurs at the end of the paragraph. Occasionally you may find a paragraph in which the topic sentence is clearly suggested but not directly stated. However, as you prepare to take the OGT, you should always put the topic sentence in writing.

Each body paragraph has its own main idea and focus. The main idea is expressed in a topic sentence. The other sentences provide focus by explaining or supporting the topic sentence. Think of the structure of each body paragraph this way:

In outline format:

Topic sentence
—Supporting fact, detail, or opinion
—Supporting fact, detail, or opinion
—Supporting fact, detail, or opinion

In paragraph format:

Topic sentence. First supporting fact, detail, or opinion expressed in one or two sentences. Second supporting fact, detail, or opinion expressed in one or two sentences. Third supporting fact, detail, or opinion expressed in one or two sentences.

All the body paragraphs, taken together, present the key ideas that develop your paper's thesis fully. To move from one idea to the next, either within or between paragraphs, you can use transitions.

- A *transition* is a word, phrase, or sentence that helps move the reader's attention smoothly from one idea to the next. Transitions help your reader see the connections between your ideas by explaining the relationships between them. For examples of transitions, study the table on pages 45–46.

Conclusion

You introduced your topic and thesis in the introduction, and you developed your thesis in the body paragraphs. In the conclusion, you have two main goals:

1. to tie together all the ideas to emphasize the validity of your thesis
2. to give closure to the paper

For instance, if your paper argues that readers should take a particular action, restate what that action is. Emphasize why that action is necessary or important. If your paper includes three or four key ideas in support of your thesis, you can briefly summarize those ideas again and then make a statement about their significance.

For examples of words and phrases that help sum up ideas and give closure, study the section called "Summarize or bring to a close" in the table on page 46.

Study the sample informative essay that follows. It illustrates the typical structure of a paper: introduction, body, and conclusion. Notice how ideas and information are organized within the paragraphs. Notice, too, how the introduction informs readers of the thesis and how the conclusion gives closure.

School is a place where every young teenager spends a great deal of time. At school, our minds are fed, but so are our bodies and hearts. A truly great school has strong academics for the mind, but it also offers opportunities in sports (for the body) and social activities (for the heart). West Wright High is exactly this kind of quality school. At WWH, a student gets a great education, preparing for graduation and college. But also, each student finds athletic teams, exciting clubs, and entertaining student-oriented events.

At WWH, academics are our top priority. Students enjoy small class sizes. As a result, we have plenty of opportunity to ask questions in class and get extra help if we need it. Teachers are friendly and care about the

This paragraph is the introduction. It begins by identifying the topic in a general way (school); then it gets specific about WWH and what it offers. The strong "hook" (sentence 2) gets the reader's interest. The last two sentences state the thesis of the paper.

The paragraph begins with a topic sentence stating the paragraph's main idea, academics.

students and the school. For advanced learners, there is an AP track offering advanced placement English and math. Excellence in academics is encouraged by our tradition of competing academically in the University Interscholastic League.

> The other sentences give specific details to support the topic. Since every detail relates to academics, the paragraph is focused.

After a hard day in class, most students enjoy playing or watching sports. At WWH, you can choose from basketball, baseball, softball, football, and volleyball. Each year, at least a couple of our teams place well in playoffs, and they have developed a devoted following from townsfolk. WWH students show team spirit by painting their faces in the school colors, blue and gold.

> This paragraph begins with a transition to help ideas move smoothly from "class" to "sports." Specific sports are named, plus details about playoffs and fans. All details relate to sports, giving the paragraph focus.

In addition to sports, WWH students enjoy taking part in clubs. The drama club puts on two plays a year, and the writing club publishes a magazine of student work each semester. Members of our chess club have competed with other clubs around the state, both in person and over the Internet. Our math club attracts guest speakers from the local college. And last but not least, the music club has helped develop talented singers and musicians who earn college music scholarships.

> In addition is a nice transition. The topic sentence (sentence 1) is supported by details about drama, writing, chess, math, and music. Notice that the writer did more than just list the clubs—she gave a memorable detail about each.

Even a school with great academics, sports, and clubs is not complete without special events. At WWH, dances are scheduled throughout the year, including the ever popular spring prom. Pep rallies give students a chance to vent their excitement about teams and to scream and shout for a good reason. One of our most popular events is the Fall Carnival, complete with games, food, a cakewalk, and a bake-off. One unique event is the annual Wright Brothers Parade, which students put on in honor of Orville and Wilbur Wright, who grew up not far from here.

> This paragraph begins with a sophisticated transition. It not only moves the reader's thoughts smoothly from the previous paragraph to this one but gives unity to the paper by bringing together the key ideas—academics, sports, clubs, and special events. Notice that each body paragraph is developed with about the same amount of detail.

Academics, sports, clubs, and events—these four things make a school worth giving your all to. In return, WWH gives its students memories and experiences that stay with them for a lifetime.

In the sample essay above, you'll notice two main strengths: First, the entire essay **focuses** on one main idea (what WWH offers students). Second, the writing is **coherent** (clear and logical).

Focus and Coherence

Focused writing

- ☑ Centers on one main idea
- ☑ Each paragraph supports that main idea
- ☑ Maintains consistent sense of audience and purpose

Coherent writing

- ☑ Has a clear, logical structure
- ☑ Flows logically from one idea or detail to the next
- ☑ Uses transitions to show relationships between ideas

You saw a few transitions in the sample paper. To learn more transitions, study the table that follows.

Transitional Words and Phrases

TO DO THIS . . .	USE . . .
Give an example	for example, for instance, such as, one reason, specifically, in particular, namely, to illustrate

Add information	and, also, in addition, another, besides, too, as well, moreover, next, what's more
Show effect, consequence, or conclusion	as a result, consequently, therefore, because of, for this reason, thus
Compare	similarly, likewise, both, at the same time, in the same way
Contrast	but, yet, in contrast, however, although, even though, while, otherwise, on the other hand, on the contrary, nevertheless, instead
Emphasize	most important, in particular, primarily, in fact, especially, above all, even more, obviously
Show sequence or time	first, second, third, next, after, before, soon, immediately, while, during, later, then, meanwhile, after a while, at last, last, finally, ultimately, in the past, in the future, since then, at the same time
Show place or direction	over, under, beside, around, nearby, close, far, in the distance, farther, closer, in front of, inside, outside, above, below, to the left, to the right
Summarize or bring to a close	in summary, to sum up, finally, last, in conclusion, for these reasons, to conclude, on the whole, in other words, in general, after all

3: Revising and Editing

A rough draft is called "rough" for a reason. It needs smoothing and polishing to prepare it for the final step, publication.

When you write a paper for the OGT, plan to leave time for revising and editing the draft. At this stage, you'll check to make sure your thesis is clear, the paper is well organized, and the writing is focused and coherent. You'll also pay special attention to the writing conventions of spelling, punctuation, capitalization, and grammar.

When you revise, you'll focus on the **structure** and **coherence** of your writing. You may make some big changes, move sentences around, cross out sentences, and add details during this stage. After the larger changes are made, you'll focus on smaller (but equally important) changes when you edit errors in **writing conventions**. You will learn more about these conventions in Lessons 2 and 3 of this book.

Structure and Coherence

Clarity of main idea. Is my main idea crystal clear? Is my thesis specific and clear? Does each paragraph focus on one idea in support of the main idea? Is my purpose clear?

Logic. Is there a clear connection between main ideas and supporting details? Have I used transitions to clarify relationships between ideas and sentences?

Style and sentence structure. Have I used a mixture of sentences types and lengths? Have I let my own voice shine through in my sentence style and word choices?

Always use complete sentences, unless you are using a fragment for a specific purpose (such as in dialogue).

Word choice. Have I used words correctly according to the meaning I intend? Have I used standard English? If I used slang or informal English, does it have a purpose (such as dialogue in a narrative)?

Choose vivid, specific words over dull, overused ones. For example, *very, really, nice, interesting,* and *fun* tend to be overused and are dull. Fresher choices are *extremely, certainly, enjoyable, remarkable,* and *entertaining,* to name a few. Each time you notice a dull word popping up in your writing as you prepare for the OGT, grab a thesaurus and learn some synonyms to use instead.

Transitions. Have I used transitional words or phrases to make ideas and relationships clear and logical?

Become familiar with the table of transitional words and phrases, and choose a few favorites to remember and use. Your choice of transitions adds to your personal style.

Legible writing. Is my writing legible?

Erase (or cross out) and rewrite any word that the scorer may not be able to read. You can't get credit for what can't be read. Remember, you can use cursive or printing to write your test.

Writing Conventions

Spelling. Have I used correct spelling?

Even though you cannot use a dictionary during the Writing Test, you can check for spelling errors you recognize, such as writing *their* when you meant *they're* or writing *nieghbor* when you meant *neighbor*.

Punctuation and capitalization. Have I used correct punctuation and capitalization?

Make sure every sentence has end punctuation (period, exclamation mark, question mark). Check your use of commas, apostrophes, colons, and semicolons. Begin every sentence and proper nouns with capital letters.

Grammar. Have I used correct grammar?

Make sure you use the parts of speech correctly. For instance, use consistent verb tense throughout the paper; do not switch from past tense to present tense for no reason. Place modifying words, phrases, and clauses as closely as possible to the words they modify in order to avoid a misunderstanding. Make sure that items in a list are written in parallel structure—for example, all verbs or all adjective phrases, but not a mix of verbs and adjective phrases.

The following checklist sums up the main areas to revise and edit. Become familiar with this checklist and use it whenever you write for OGT practice or class work.

Editing Checklist

Structure and Coherence

- ❏ Clarity of Main Idea
- ❏ Focus on audience and purpose
- ❏ Logic
- ❏ Style and Sentence Structure
- ❏ Word Choice
- ❏ Transitions

Writing Conventions

- ❏ Spelling
- ❏ Punctuation and Capitalization
- ❏ Grammar

Now examine the following rough paragraphs that have been revised using the editing checklist. The words in the column to the right identify the kinds of revisions made.

Of all the schools in town, West Wright
High has the nicest campus.
∧There is a jogging path around the edge of the WWH
                  and along   charming
campus;, Along the path are ~~pretty~~ trees, shrubs and flowers;, ¢ared   c

for by the horticulture club. At the back of the campus is a duck
                                                Beside it are
pond that has been there since before the campus was built.∧Picnic   P
              where   their
tables ~~are out there~~, students eat ~~there~~ lunches ~~at the tables~~ and do

homework.

        The big fountain out front/ ~~It~~ adds an artistic touch to the
    appearance   is a surprising source of generosity and fun
school's ~~look~~ and ~~makes the school more welcoming to come to every~~
          ∧All   is
~~day.~~ ⟨all⟩ the money tossed into the fountain ~~are~~ donated to the
                h
children's ∧ospital in town. Sometimes as a prank students squirts

dishwashing liquid into the fountain to make huge piles of bubbles.
Although   al   it's   who
∧The principle hates this;, ~~Its~~ fun for the students,, ~~They~~ have bubble   t

wars and come to class covered in soap.

| clarity of main idea; sentence structure; word choice; sentence structure |

| transitional words; spelling |

| sentence structure; logic; capitalization; grammar; capitalization; grammar |

| transition; spelling; sentence structure |

Do the changes reflect how you would have revised the paragraphs?
Maybe not, and that's okay. Remember that revision choices are a sign
of your personal writing style, and you may edit and improve a rough
draft one way, while someone else would make different changes.
What's most important is that the final product is correct, clear, logical,
focused, and engaging to read.

Revise a Paragraph
Revise and polish the paragraph that follows. Use the editing checklist
and sample revision above to guide and inspire you. To make your
changes, you may cross out and rewrite, use editing marks, or use a
combination of the two techniques.

West Wright High's newest club are the computer club. It held it's first meeting during the first semester of this scool year. Only a handful of students attended. Now members total thirty-six. Popularity growing. Almost everyone in town has access to a computer these days. One of their first projects was to create a good Web site to show everyone what they can do. Programmers wrote the code, and a few student-artists created nice computer-generated art. On the main page club members has personal links. there personal pages show personal interests. Poems, computer art, photos, stories, and other personal interests.

4: Publishing

The final stage of your writing process is publication, which is when your work goes public. When you write papers for the OGT Writing, publication will consist simply of turning in your work to the teacher in charge. Similarly, when you write papers for classes, you'll "publish" them by submitting them to your teacher. Other ways of publishing your work include showing the work to friends and family members, submitting the work to a school or city newspaper, posting it on a Web site, or submitting it to an employer. In fact, throughout your life you will be publishing your writing in one manner or another, whether it is for school, work, or personal reasons.

Respond to a Writing Prompt
Follow the numbered steps to complete the process of writing your own paper.

1. Reading the Writing Prompt
Read the writing prompt in the box below. After the prompt is space for you to note the topic, purpose, and audience for your paper.

TOPIC FOR WRITING

> Movie theaters in your town are considering a new policy. If they establish this policy, anyone under age sixteen must be accompanied by a parent or guardian to attend any movie, regardless of its rating. Take a position; then write a letter to the manager of Cinema Association persuading him or her to agree with your viewpoint on this policy.

Topic: _____

Purpose: _____

Audience: _____

Form: _____

2. Prewriting

On a piece of paper, make a plan for a response to the writing prompt. Remember, prewriting is not scored, but prewriting is essential to planning and organizing a top-score writing sample. Therefore, you should give prewriting your best effort. You may want to review the section on prewriting techniques on pages 34–40.

3. Writing

Write your rough draft on a separate sheet of paper. Use your prewriting notes to guide your writing. *Hint:* Since this prompt asks for a letter written to "the manager of Cinema Association," begin your draft by writing "Dear Cinema Association Manager:" Then proceed with structured, focused paragraphs. After your conclusion, write "Sincerely, (your name)."

4. Revising and Editing

Revise and edit your rough draft. Make your changes directly on the draft. You may want to refer to the section on revising and editing on pages 46–50.

5. Publishing

Submit your finished paper to your teacher according to his or her directions. Your teacher may ask you to exchange papers with a classmate in order to discuss your writing process and the finished result with a partner.

Respond to the writing prompt. First plan your response on a piece of paper. This section will not be scored. Write your draft on separate, lined paper. The draft needs to be legible, and you may use cursive or printed handwriting. Revise and edit your draft, making your changes directly on the draft itself.

TOPIC FOR WRITING

> A friend has commented to you that beauty is in the eye of the beholder. Explain to your friend what, in your opinion, makes a person beautiful. Be specific in your explanation.

Look & Learn

We relate to our world through stories. We say to our friends, "Let me tell you about what happened to me." We refer to our lives as stories—"the story of my life." We read novels (printed stories), we watch movies (filmed stories), we attend plays ("live" stories), and we watch sitcoms, cartoons, soap operas, and TV movies (more stories!).

The OGT Writing may require you to write a narrative about a given topic. As with the persuasive and informative prompts, the given topic will help get you started, but you will develop the ideas and details yourself. For instance, the prompt may guide you to write a *story*, which has characters and plot and whose main purpose is entertainment. Or the prompt may guide you to write a *narrative essay*, which has characters and plot but whose main purpose is to communicate a theme or message. The prompt will typically ask you to write a narrative based on your own experiences.

Your narrative will be scored using the same standards as those used to score informative and persuasive writing. You can turn to pages 27–28 to review the **rubrics** for a top-score response on the OGT Writing.

As you did when responding to informative and persuasive writing prompts in Lesson 1.2, you will use the **writing process** when responding to narrative prompts. The OGT Writing will include pages for pre-writing and writing, and you will revise and edit right there on the draft.

So now you know about the scoring standards and the writing process. You may be wondering at this point about **content**. What are you expected to put in your narrative? Take a look at the learning benchmark that the Ohio Department of Education has developed to describe your narrative writing goal:

In the Spotlight

Narrative Writing Benchmark

Compose narratives that establish a specific setting, plot and a consistent point of view, and develop characters by using sensory details and concrete language.

Let's take a closer look at the elements listed in the learning benchmark.

- **Setting:** the time and place of the events

- **Plot:** the conflict, rising action, climax, and resolution. The plot may incorporate literary devices such as foreshadowing and flashback.

- **Point of view:** the perspective from which the narrative is told, most often first-person point of view

- **Characters:** the people or creatures in your story, made real through sensory details (sight, feel, taste, touch, smell) and concrete language (specific details)

Think about these four narrative elements as you read the following writing prompt. Do you have any ideas about how you'd respond to this prompt with a narrative that includes setting, plot, point of view, and characters?

TOPIC FOR WRITING

Write a story about a birthday party. Tell where the party was and what happened. Develop your story with details.

As you learned in Lesson 1.2, the first step in your planning (prewriting) stage is reading the prompt and determining exactly what it asks for. In the prompt above, the signal word "story" tells you this is a narrative writing prompt (not persuasive or expository). The prompt also gives you the freedom to tell about a real event or one you make up. The rest of the prompt reminds you to include the elements of setting, plot, and details.

Since writing a narrative requires you to generate details about characters, setting, conflict, and plot, your prewriting is especially important. Prewriting will not be graded, so give yourself permission to let your ideas flow without worrying about how they might sound to someone else. Grammar, punctuation, and spelling will matter later, but they don't matter at this point.

One prewriting technique you might try is to sketch a children's slide—yes, a slide like you see in a playground!—and use it to develop your plot. Here is an example of how you can use the slide to shape a plot in response to the prompt above.

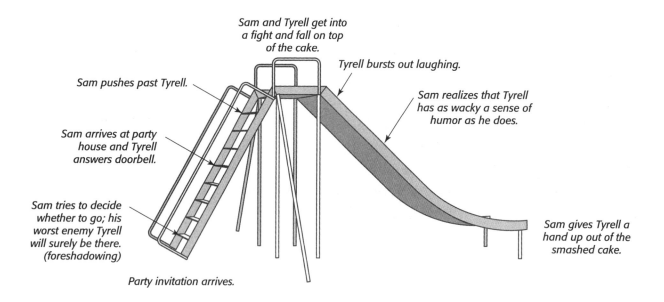

Sam and Tyrell get into a fight and fall on top of the cake.

Tyrell bursts out laughing.

Sam pushes past Tyrell.

Sam realizes that Tyrell has as wacky a sense of humor as he does.

Sam arrives at party house and Tyrell answers doorbell.

Sam tries to decide whether to go; his worst enemy Tyrell will surely be there. (foreshadowing)

Sam gives Tyrell a hand up out of the smashed cake.

Party invitation arrives.

After the planning stage comes the writing stage. Take a look at the following draft of a narrative based on the prewriting about Sam and Tyrell.

Birthday Party Surprise

When Sam opened Hannah's birthday party invitation, his freckled face broke into a grin. Fantastic! Then his grin faded. Hannah was sure to invite Tyrell. The problem? He and Tyrell were hot and cold, north and south, right and left—in other words, complete opposites. He would rather eat dirt alone than eat birthday cake with Tyrell.

Nevertheless, Sam was on Hannah's doorstep on the party day. Through the door floated sounds of music and laughter. Clearly, everyone was having a good time. But would he have a good time if Tyrell were inside?

Suddenly, with a swoosh, the door opened. Tyrell stood there grinning like the cat that ate the canary.

Sam pushed past Tyrell into Hannah's living room. Ah! The refreshment table. Punch would cool him off—he hoped.

Just as he lifted the punch ladle, someone jostled his arm. Tyrell! Sam watched as green punch splashed on the tablecloth like spilled alien guts. Without another thought, he shoved Tyrell with his shoulder.

foreshadowing

metaphor

hyperbole

third-person narration

the setting

suspense

rising action

a simile

more rising action

a simile

In a flash both boys crashed into the table. The cake met the floor with a wet splat. Worse, Sam and Tyrell landed on top of the sticky mess.

Then peals of laughter rang out. Glancing sideways, Sam saw Tyrell, his black, curly hair decorated with pink-frosting roses. He looked ridiculous—but he knew it and was laughing at himself!

Sam eyed Tyrell. Anyone with a sense of humor like that couldn't be all bad. He stood and held out a hand to Tyrell. "Need a hand, friend?" he said.

the climax
onomatopoeia

falling action
concrete language to characterize Tyrell

the resolution

As with persuasive and expository papers, save a little time at the end of your writing period to revise and edit your draft. Use the editing and revising strategies you studied in Lesson 1.2. For your reference, here is the editing checklist.

Editing Checklist

Structure and Coherence

❑ Clarity of Main Idea
❑ Focus on audience and purpose
❑ Logic
❑ Style and Sentence Structure
❑ Word Choice
❑ Transitions

Writing Conventions

❑ Spelling
❑ Punctuation and Capitalization
❑ Grammar

Respond to a Narrative Writing Prompt

Remember that you may be asked to write either a *story* or a *narrative essay*. While a story may be true or imagined, a narrative essay describes a real-life event or experience from the first-person point of view.

Follow the numbered steps to complete the process of writing your own narrative. Use the prewriting strategy illustrated on page 54 to plan your response.

1. Read the Writing Prompt

Read the writing prompt in the box below. After the prompt is space for you to note the topic, purpose, and audience for your response.

TOPIC FOR WRITING

Write a narrative essay about a challenge you have faced in life, such as accepting a new stepsibling or dealing with a difficult individual at school. Write the essay to appeal to readers of your own age. Tell where the events take place and what happens. Develop your essay with details.

Topic: _____

Purpose: _____

Audience: _____

2. Prewrite

Use the following diagram to help plan the parts of your story. Use additional sheets of your own paper for additional planning, organizing, and idea-generating activities.

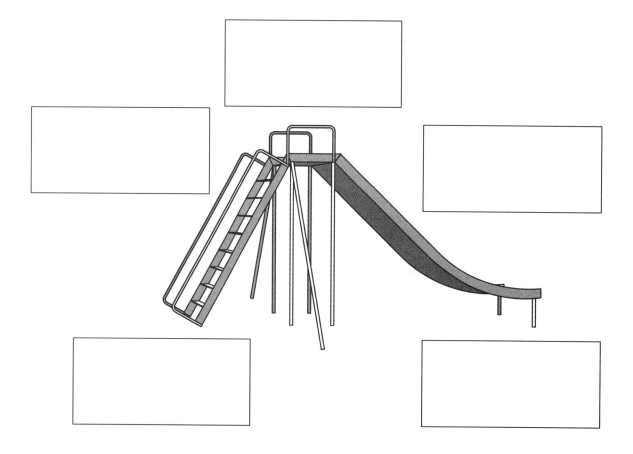

3. Write

Write your narrative on separate, lined paper.

4. Revise and Edit

Revise and edit your narrative. In addition to using the Editing Checklist, use this Narrative Checklist.

Narrative Checklist

Did I Include . . .

❑ a specific setting?

❑ a well-developed plot, including rising action with conflict/ tension, a climax, and a resolution?

❑ characters made real through sensory details (sight, smell, hearing, taste, touch) and concrete language (details about appearance, mannerisms, etc.)?

❑ a consistent point of view?

❑ correct spelling, punctuation, capitalization, and grammar?

As you revise and edit, make your changes directly on the draft to be scored.

5. Publish

Publish your writing by giving it to one or more readers, such as classmates or your teacher. Get feedback on your narrative's setting, plot, characters, point of view, and writing conventions. For extra practice, revise the narrative again based on the feedback that you received. Think about how you can use some of these new revision ideas next time you write a narrative.

Respond to the following writing topic. Use your own paper for prewriting and for writing the draft. You may use printed or cursive handwriting. Revise and edit by erasing, crossing out, or making other changes on the draft itself.

TOPIC FOR WRITING

Your school is publishing a collection of holiday stories to send out to families in the community. For the collection, write a narrative about a holiday celebration. Tell where the celebration took place and what happened. Develop your story with details.

Quick Review: The Writing Process

Prewriting is the first stage of the writing process. First, you read and decode the prompt to understand what it is asking for: What is the topic? Should your writing sample be expository? Persuasive? A narrative? Next, you develop ideas about the topic by brainstorming or gathering information, and consider ways to organize it. You may use lists, graphic organizers, outlines, sentences, questions and answers, or other forms you find helpful.

Writing is the second stage of the process, when you form sentences and paragraphs to express ideas, persuade readers, or tell a story. You organize your sentences and paragraphs in a format appropriate to the writing purpose—whether an essay, a letter, a narrative, or other form.

Revising and editing constitute the third stage of writing, when you go over the draft to correct errors, reword sentences, or make other changes to improve structure and meaning.

Publishing is the final stage of writing, when you present the draft to the intended audience.

DIRECTIONS: Write a complete, edited response to each of the following two writing topics.

You may start with either topic; divide your time as you think appropriate. Plan your writing either in the space provided or on a piece of paper. Your prewriting is an important part of the writing process and should be completed, but it will not be scored. Write the drafts that you want scored on your own lined paper. These drafts should be legible; they may be in printed or in cursive handwriting.

Revise and edit your writing. Erasing, crossing out, and other editing changes may be made right on the drafts themselves.

TOPIC FOR WRITING #1

It has been said that the only difference between children and adults is the price of their toys. Explain what toys you enjoy and which ones you plan never to give up. Be specific in your explanation.

TOPIC FOR WRITING #2

Each year the Student Council holds a food and clothing drive to raise money for a good cause. This year, council members must decide on one of the following causes: homeless shelter, senior citizens' center, animal shelter, or environmental cleanup. To which cause do you think the money should go? Write a letter to the Student Council president, persuading him or her to see your point of view. Be specific in developing your argument.

PART THREE

Using Correct Writing Conventions

Writing Conventions Benchmarks

A. Use correct spelling conventions.
B. Use correct punctuation and capitalization.

> *Romeo and Juliet*
> *peanut butter and jelly*
> *day and night*

Every day we encounter word pairs like those above. Each element in the duo seems more complete, more meaningful, when used together. Written communication is a lot like that. On one hand you have the message of the writing, and on the other hand you have the nuts and bolts, the technique of how that message is put into words. In the best writing, a strong combination of message (words) and technique (writing conventions) communicates meaning from writer to reader.

Writing conventions include spelling, punctuation, capitalization, and grammar. In Lesson 2, you'll focus on the first three items in this list, while Lesson 3 focuses on grammar. Lesson 2 gives you the opportunity to review the basic rules of spelling, punctuation, and capitalization. You will also practice recognizing and correcting errors in these conventions.

Rules for the writing conventions are very detailed, so don't expect to remember all of them after one reading. Review and practice are the keys to success. Give yourself permission to review and practice as often as it takes to become familiar with using the conventions correctly.

The OGT Writing will test your understanding of the conventions in three ways. First, you must be able to *apply* the rules when you write your essays. Second, you must show your *understanding* of the rules when you edit and revise as part of the writing process. Finally, you must be able to *identify* the rules in order to correctly revise and edit for the short-answer question.

Look & Learn

Let's face it. Learning to spell correctly can be a challenge. The English language is notorious for its silent letters, homonyms, pronunciations that look nothing like the spellings, and other roadblocks on the path to spelling correctly all the time. So if you think spelling is sometimes difficult, that's okay. It is difficult for most people, and some words continue to challenge writers even after they have extensive education. That's why you'll find dictionaries on classroom shelves and in university professors' offices, businesses, and homes everywhere.

Challenging though it may be, spelling is crucial to communicating well. Job applications, school papers, college applications, business memos—no matter what you're writing, your ideas will be taken more seriously if you spell correctly. Starting right now, you can improve your spelling in several ways.

50 Commonly Misspelled Words to Study

- absence
- achievement
- all right
- a lot
- answered
- argument
- beginning
- believe
- business
- chief
- conscience
- coming
- definitely
- dependent
- embarrass
- February
- finally
- friend
- grammar
- guess
- happiness
- heroes
- judgment
- likable
- minuscule
- necessary
- noticeable
- occurred
- occurrence
- often
- persuade
- pursue
- scene

In the Spotlight

- **Read.** Your ability to recognize a word spelled correctly (or incorrectly) is related to your familiarity with words in print. Reading and noticing how words are spelled will strengthen your spelling skills.

- **Write.** Writing down a word spelled correctly helps train your brain to remember how to spell the word the next time you write it. If you find that you consistently misspell certain words, practice writing them correctly. When you encounter new vocabulary, write those words to get the feel for how they are spelled, letter by letter.

- **Know spelling rules.** You can find spelling rules in language handbooks and language textbooks. In this book, this lesson reviews rules of spelling.

- **Use dictionaries.** Any time you are unsure of the spelling of a word, look it up in a dictionary. Look for it in each of the ways you think it is spelled until you find it. However, be sure to read the definition to make sure the word has the meaning you think it does. Be aware of homophones—words that sound alike but have different spellings, such as *ball* and *bawl*, *there* and *their*, *its* and *it's*.

This lesson reviews words commonly confused.

Spelling Rules

Commonly Misspelled Words (continued)

separate
since
solely
straight
subtle
sugar
tear
therefore
though
tonight
Tuesday
usually
weight
weird
whether
whole
women

1. Writing *ie* and *ei*

(a) Write *i* before *e* when the sound is long *e*, except after *c*.

Examples   niece, chief, field, conceit, receipt, ceiling, brief, achieve

Exceptions   seize, neither, protein, weird, species

(b) Write *e* before *i* when the sound is not long *e*.

Examples   neighbor, sleigh, foreign, eight, height, freight, weigh, heir

Exceptions   patience, experience, friend, ancient, mischief

2. Adding prefixes

When adding a prefix, do not change the spelling of the original word.

Examples   un + pack = unpack   un + natural = unnatural
             dis + ability = disability   il + legal = illegal

3. Adding suffixes

(a) When adding -*ly* or -*ness,* do not change the spelling of the original word.

Examples   loud + ly = loudly   famous + ly = famously
             beautiful + ly = beautifully   clean + ness = cleanness
             handsome + ness = handsomeness

Exceptions to this rule usually involve words ending in *y* or *ll.*
             angry + ly = angrily   full + ly = fully
             silly + ness = silliness

(b) When the original word ends in silent *e* . . .
. . . drop the *e* to add a suffix beginning with a vowel.

Examples   erase + able = erasable   compete + ing = competing
             joke + er = joker   cute + est = cutest
Exceptions   mile + age = mileage   dye + ing = dyeing

. . . keep the *e* to add a suffix beginning with a consonant.

Examples   hate + ful = hateful   sole + ly = solely
             safe + ty = safety
Exceptions   true + ly = truly   nine + th = ninth
             whole + ly = wholly

(c) When the original word ends in a vowel and *y,* keep the *y* when adding a suffix.

Examples   enjoy + able = enjoyable   play + ing = playing
joy + ous = joyous
Exceptions day + ly = daily   pay + ed = paid

(d) When the original word ends in a consonant and *y*, change the *y* to *i* before a suffix not beginning with *i*.

Examples   funny + er = funnier   plenty + ful = plentiful
carry + ing = carrying
Exceptions shy + er = shyer   dry + ly = dryly

Identify Correct Spelling

In each sentence, underline the correct spelling of the word in parentheses.

Example   Sometimes, fact is *(truely, truly)* stranger than fiction.

1. *(Terrifying, Terriffying)* dragons that feast on human beings are fiction, right?
2. Not *(exactely, exactly)*.
3. *(Wieghing, Weighing)* up to three hundred pounds, the Komodo dragon of Indonesia has been known to chase down and attack people—and eat them.
4. Such (viciousness, vicioussness) is directed at its own kind, too.
5. *(Occasionally, Occasionaly)* Komodo dragons devour each other.
6. Newly hatched *(babys, babies)*, measuring about eighteen inches, live in trees for several months.
7. Perhaps this *(unusual, unnusual)* nursery provides safety from hungry adults.
8. Its teeth are *(certainely, certainly)* dangerous.
9. However, the Komodo dragon's filthy mouth can cause death *(indirectly, inndirectly)*.
10. Its mouth is filled with *(microorganisms, microrganisms)*.
11. Also called germs, these microscopic creatures cause infection in the dragon's *(biten, bitten)* prey.
12. Even if the bite doesn't kill, the infection can, *(producing, produceing)* the dragon's favorite meal—dead flesh.
13. This is an *(amazeing, amazing)* reptile.
14. Technically, however, it is a lizard, not a *(biollogical, biological)* dragon.

15. Large and long-lived, it can grow up to ten feet long, *(living, live-ing)* 100 years.

4. Writing plurals

(a) To make most words plural, add *s*.

Examples   heart, hearts   bottle, bottles   cake, cakes
                 river, rivers   actor, actors

(b) For words ending in *s, sh, ss, ch, x,* or *z,* add *es*.

Examples   glass, glasses   crash, crashes   lunch, lunches
                 box, boxes   fuzz, fuzzes

(c) For words ending in a consonant and *o,* add *es*.

Examples   hero, heroes   tomato, tomatoes   torpedo, torpedoes
Exceptions piano, pianos   zero, zeros

(d) For words ending in a vowel and *o,* add *s*.

Examples   patio, patios   kangaroo, kangaroos   rodeo, rodeos
                 ratio, ratios

(e) For some nouns ending in *f* or *fe,* add *s*. For others, change the *f* or *fe* to *v* and add *es*.

Examples   roof, roofs   belief, beliefs   wife, wives
                 hoof, hooves

(f) For words ending in a consonant and *y,* change the *y* to *i* and add *es*.

Examples   theory, theories   canary, canaries   ninety, nineties
                 cry, cries

(g) Some words form their plurals irregularly.

Examples   man, men   bacterium, bacteria   foot, feet
                 tooth, teeth   deer, deer   child, children
                 datum, data   woman, women   alga, algae
                 moose, moose basis, bases   series, series

Tip

Do not use an apostrophe to make words plural.

Example   schools = plural of school
              school's = possessive form of school

Spell Plurals Correctly

Write the plural of each word. If you have trouble, read the spelling rule referred to in the column to the right of the item. The first item is completed for you.

Singular	Plural	Rule
1. fox	_foxes_	4(b)
2. half		4(e)
3. movie		4(a)
4. berry		4(f)
5. taboo		4(d)
6. person		4(g)
7. potato		4(c)
8. reproach		4(b)
9. tax		4(b)
10. proof		4(e)
11. calf		4(e)
12. piano		4(c)
13. country		4(f)
14. success		4(b)
15. mouse		4(g)

Common Spelling Mistakes

Some words tend to be misspelled more often than others. Often the misspelling occurs because unpronounced letters or syllables are left out, or words that sound alike are confused with each other.

Unpronounced Letters or Syllables

In casual speech, we may not pronounce certain letters or syllables in some words. *Government* sounds like *goverment,* and *probably* sounds like *probly.* In other words, some letters are silent, as in *foreign.* With both types of words, it is helpful to become familiar with how the correct spelling looks in writing. As a result, you are more likely to say, "Hey, that word doesn't look right. It is misspelled."

Study the following list of words commonly misspelled. Unpronounced letters or syllables are in boldface.

accident**a**lly	Feb**r**uary	mus**c**le
a**dj**ective	fore**i**gn	proba**b**ly
can**di**date	frien**d**ship	quanti**t**y
clo**th**es	gene**r**ally	resta**u**rant
conde**mn**	gove**rn**ment	sep**a**rate (adjective)
di**ff**erent	han**d**book	stren**g**th
drastic**a**lly	int**e**rest	surprise
envir**o**nment	lib**r**ary	We**d**nesday

Homophones

Homophones are words that sound alike but have different spellings and meanings. *Here* and *hear* are homophones. Misspelling occurs when the writer uses the wrong spelling for the intended meaning. Other words are pronounced nearly the same, also resulting in spelling errors. Two such words are *accept* and *except*.

Study the following list of words commonly confused.

accept	To receive. *I accept your apology.*
except	To leave out. *I like all fruits except bananas.*
affect	To influence. *Your opinion will affect my decision.*
effect	(v.) To cause to happen. *Bacteria and fungi effect decay of dead matter.*
	(n.) A result. *What effect did the flood have in your town?*
buy	To purchase. *Please buy cat food today.*
by	Next to; through. *The front desk by the window is mine.*
capital	Main city. *The capital of Ohio is Columbus.*
capitol	Legislators' building. *The capitol has flags out front and a dome on top.*
its	Possessive of *it*. *The elm tree drops its leaves in autumn.*
it's	Contraction of *it is*. *Mrs. King said, "It's time for a pop quiz!"*
principal	Head of a school. *The principal spoke at the tenth-grade assembly.*
	Main; most important. *The principal cause of the fight was name-calling.*
principle	Basic truth; code of conduct. *Our friendship is founded on the principle of honesty.*
their	Possessive of *they*. *They spent their weekend at my house.*
there	At that place. *Please leave your muddy shoes there.*
they're	Contraction of *they are*. *They're arriving on the six o'clock train.*
to	A preposition. *Did you send an invitation to Aunt Jennifer?*
	Part of the infinitive form of a verb. *Dad is learning to use a computer.*
too	Also. *We grilled chicken, and we grilled vegetables too.*
two	The number between one and three. *My two favorite colors are blue and purple.*
who's	Contraction of *who is*. *Who's at the door?*
whose	Possessive of *who*. *I don't know whose football this is.*
your	Possessive of *you*. *Where did you rent your tuxedo?*
you're	Contraction of *you are*. *I love you because you're fun, honest, and loyal.*

More Homophones and Commonly Confused Words

advice, advise	heard, herd
altar, alter	hoarse, horse
bare, bear	know, no
board, bored	loose, lose
brake, break	passed, past
cite, sight, site	peace, piece
coarse, course	plain, plane
complement, compliment	presence, presents
conscience, conscious	rain, rein, reign
councilor, counselor	scene, seen
desert, dessert	stationary, stationery
die, dye	than, then
fair, fare	through, thorough, threw
forth, fourth	weak, week
hear, here	weather, whether

Correct Spelling Errors

Correct the spelling errors (one per item). Some items have no errors.

Example   I would love to play golf, but I can't afford to ~~by~~ the

buy (above "by")

equipment.

1. I generally do research for school papers in the city libary.

2. Did you brake your arm during that crash on your skateboard?

3. The clerk said, "Let me know if you're intrested in items behind the counter."

4. I heard you won fourth place in the short story contest. Congratulations!

5. "Go straight to the principal's office" are never good words to here.

6. Hector accidentally broke a neighbor's window with a baseball.

7. Did you hear? The suprise birthday party for Megan was fantastic!

8. I'm making an egg salad sandwich. Do you want one to?

9. Listening to classical music has a calming affect on my mood.

10. In the past Liam was really shy, but lately he has gained confidence.

In the passage below, certain words are underlined and numbered. Following the passage are alternative spellings for each underlined word. For each one, select the letter of the correct spelling. If no change is needed, choose A for NO CHANGE.

Pop Art

During the 1950s and '60s, artists developed an

art style called pop art (short for popular art). In this

<u>intresting</u> art form, painters, sculptors, and other kinds
1

     1. **A.** NO CHANGE
        B. interesting
        C. intiresting
        D. enteresting

of artists drew <u>there</u> <u>inspration</u> from popular culture.
       2   3

     2. **A.** NO CHANGE
        B. they're
        C. ther
        D. their

     3. **A.** NO CHANGE
        B. insperation
        C. inspiration
        D. inspraition

Comic strips, <u>advertisements</u>, billboards, and other
               4

images related to brand names showed up in artistic

creations.

     4. **A.** NO CHANGE
        B. advertisments
        C. advertisemints
        D. avertisements

    <u>Fore example</u>, Roy Lichtenstein's *Nurse*, an oil and
       5

magna on canvas, shows a woman nurse's head and

     5. **A.** NO CHANGE
        B. Four example
        C. Foar example
        D. For example

shoulders in cartoon style, <u>creating</u> the <u>affect</u> of being a
                   6   7

     6. **A.** NO CHANGE
        B. createing
        C. crating
        D. criating

     7. **A.** NO CHANGE
        B. effect
        C. afect
        D. efect

newspaper clipping. Many pop art <u>peaces</u> feature
8

_____ 8. **A.** NO CHANGE
     B. pieces
     C. peeces
     D. peacis

representations of <u>plane</u>, everyday objects such as
9

pencils, clothespins, and telephones. Claes Oldenberg's

_____ 9. **A.** NO CHANGE
     B. playne
     C. plain
     D. plan

Clothespin, a forty-five-foot-high <u>steal</u> sculpture, is a
10

clothespin in gigantic proportions. The pop art

movement helped to expand artists' subject matter.

_____ 10. **A.** NO CHANGE
     B. stile
     C. stael
     D. steel

Short Answer
Use the checklist to answer the following question.

Writer's Checklist

✓ Spelling plurals
✓ Adding prefixes and suffixes
✓ Homophones

The principal liked my proposeal so much that he excepted my plan and said he would implement it in the coming months.

You have been asked by a fellow student to peer edit the above sentence. Using the checklist, give the writer feedback by identifying the two rules that apply to the spelling errors in the sentence. Then rewrite the sentence correctly.

_____

_____

_____

_____

_____

_____

_____

Sentence End Marks

As you know, a complete sentence ends in one of three punctuation marks: period, question mark, or exclamation point. Depending on the end mark used, a sentence carries a particular tone and meaning. Consider the different effects created in the sentence below, just by changing the end mark.

This is a great party**.**
This is a great party**?**
This is a great party**!**

Each end mark has one or more main uses.

In the Spotlight

END MARK	USED WITH	EXAMPLE
. **period**	declarative statements	*I buried a chest of gold.*
	commands, requests	*Bury the chest of gold here.*
? **question mark**	inquiries	*Where did we bury that gold?*
! **exclamation point**	strong expressions of feeling	*Our gold was stolen!*

Use End Marks Correctly

Add an end mark to each sentence to best express its meaning and tone.

Example   What a funny story this is__!__

1. Did you hear about the purse snatcher who was working Jefferson Street____

2. Apparently, he was "accidentally" bumping into elderly women____

3. While the woman was distracted, he would grab her purse____

4. The woman usually shouted, "Stop, thief____"

5. Do you think he stopped_____

6. Well, after a dozen complaints, the police knew they had to make a plan_____

7. The captain said to an officer, "Please dress in this outfit_____"

8. The outfit was a disguise to make the officer look like a frail old woman_____

9. Imagine the purse snatcher's surprise when he tried to grab that woman's purse_____

10. He got his wrists snapped into handcuffs instead_____

The Comma (,)

Would you be surprised to know commas are misused more than any other mark of punctuation? While other punctuation marks each have one or two main purposes, the comma can serve a variety of purposes within a sentence. Careful review and practice will help you keep these uses straight. For starters, study the section below, which shows the main rules for using commas.

Using Commas

1. Use a comma before a coordinating conjunction that begins an independent clause.

Incorrect	Rodney plays basketball well but, he plays baseball even better.
Incorrect	Rodney plays basketball well but he plays baseball even better.
Incorrect	Rodney plays basketball well, he plays baseball even better. *(Do not use a comma alone to join main clauses.)*
Correct	Rodney plays basketball well**, but** he plays baseball even better.

2. Use a comma to separate items in a series.
The items may be words, phrases, or clauses.

Incorrect	The subway car came to a quick loud halt.
Correct	The subway car came to a quick**,** loud halt.
Incorrect	The ingredients are eggs cheese onions and ham.
Correct	The ingredients are eggs**,** cheese**,** onions**,** and ham.

Incorrect	I looked for you in the hallways in the classrooms and in the gym.
Correct	I looked for you in the hallways, in the classrooms, and in the gym.
Incorrect	Please tell me where you met him what his name is and how old he is.
Correct	Please tell me where you met him, what his name is, and how old he is.

Do not use a comma to separate items if you use *and* to separate them.

Incorrect	The subway car came to a quick, and loud halt.
Correct	The subway car came to a quick and loud halt.

3. Use a comma after certain introductory words, phrases, and clauses.

Incorrect	Yes I'll help with the pep squad's car wash.
Correct	Yes, I'll help with the pep squad's car wash. *(introductory word)*
Incorrect	After a night of thunder and rain the morning dawned clear and bright.
Correct	After a night of thunder and rain, the morning dawned clear and bright. *(introductory phrase)*
Incorrect	Before you eat wash your hands with soap.
Correct	Before you eat, wash your hands with soap. *(introductory clause)*

4. Use commas to set off parenthetical information.
Parenthetical information is not necessary to the main meaning of the sentence.

Incorrect	My older sister who is a college graduate is planning a June wedding.
Correct	My older sister, who is a college graduate, is planning a June wedding.

Do not use commas if the information is necessary to the main meaning of the sentence.

Incorrect	The police officer, who spoke to your class, is my uncle.
Correct	The police officer who spoke to your class is my uncle. *(The clause <u>who spoke to your class</u> is necessary to identify which officer.)*

5. Use commas to set off a noun of direct address.

Incorrect	Helen it's nice to meet you.
Correct	Helen, it's nice to meet you.

| Incorrect | It's nice to meet you Helen. |
| Correct | It's nice to meet you, Helen. |

| Incorrect | Did I tell you Helen about my parakeet? |
| Correct | Did I tell you, Helen, about my parakeet? |

> **Tip**
>
> Don't add a comma to a sentence just because you would pause there when speaking. Speech patterns do not always reflect the rules of comma usage.
>
> | Incorrect | I saw the bear at my tent, and let out a shout. |
> | Correct | I saw the bear at my tent and let out a shout. *(The two parts of the compound verb, saw and let, should not be separated by a comma because they both refer to the same subject, I.)* |

Try It Out

Use Commas Correctly

Correct the following sentences by adding or removing commas as necessary. Some sentences need no change.

Example   Many of the rules at my school, in my opinion, are

reasonable.

1. At the high school in my town we have a lot of rules.

2. It's prohibited to wear miniskirts, to use cell phones, and to go without shoes.

3. We cannot leave campus for lunch and we cannot order pizza delivered.

4. Other no-no's involve, tattoos piercings and gang colors.

5. No rulebook would be complete of course, without restricting the slogans allowed on T-shirts.

6. For example, words considered "foul language" are banned from T-shirts.

7. The purpose of all these rules is to make a safe structured environment for learning.

8. When it comes to rules, like banning weapons in school, I am in full agreement.

9. However, rules that ban pagers and handheld radios seem too strict.

10. School rules apply on campus at sports events and on school trips.

The Semicolon (;) and the Colon (:)

The **semicolon** is used to signal a brief pause—longer than a pause for a comma but not as long as that for a period. It affects the speed at which a reader moves through the sentence. A **colon** is used to point the reader's attention ahead to a list or other "announced" word or word group.

Here are a few rules for using semicolons and colons correctly.

Using the Semicolon (;)

1. Use a semicolon to join main clauses that are not connected by a coordinating conjunction.

Incorrect	Kirk's band assembled in the garage; and practice began immediately.
Correct	Kirk's band assembled in the garage**;** practice began immediately.

Do not use a semicolon to join clauses that aren't closely related in meaning.

Incorrect	Kirk's band assembled in the garage; the summer evening was warm and lazy.
Correct	Kirk's band assembled in the garage**.** The summer evening was warm and lazy.

2. Use a semicolon to join main clauses connected by a conjunctive adverb or transitional phrase.

Incorrect	Kirk's band assembled in the garage, however, Kirk himself was absent.
Correct	Kirk's band assembled in the garage**;** however, Kirk himself was absent.

Incorrect	Kirk was late arriving as a result, practice started late.
Correct	Kirk was late arriving**;** as a result, practice started late.

3. Use a semicolon to join items in a series when one or more items have a comma.

Incorrect	The band members are Kirk, my brother, Greta, his girlfriend, and Roy.
Correct	The band members are Kirk, my brother**;** Greta, his girlfriend**;** and Roy.

Coordinating Conjunctions

and, but, for, nor, or, so, yet

Conjunctive Adverbs

consequently, furthermore, however, instead, moreover, nevertheless, otherwise, therefore, thus

Transitional Phrases

as a result, for instance, in fact, on the other hand, that is

Using the Colon (:)
Use a colon to call attention to what follows.

Incorrect   My final answer is this no.

Correct   My final answer is this: no.

Incorrect   For the field trip you will need the following permission slip, sack lunch, pen, and paper.

Correct   For the field trip you'll need the following: permission slip, sack lunch, pen, and paper.

Do not use a colon between a verb and its objects.

Incorrect   For the field trip you will need: permission slip, sack lunch, pen, and paper. *(The verb <u>will need</u> takes the objects <u>permission slip</u>, <u>sack lunch</u>, <u>pen</u>, and <u>paper</u>.)*

Correct   For the field trip you will need permission slip, sack lunch, pen, and paper.

Use Semicolons and Colons Correctly
Add or remove semicolons and colons as necessary. Some sentences need no change.

Example   Some teenagers dream of owning their first car; however, I dream of owning a huge truck.

I am fascinated by powerful trucks, including semis and dump trucks. Even the parts of trucks interest me: for instance, dump truck tires can be over 12 feet high. The British have an unusual word for their largest trucks juggernauts. I enjoy reading about huge, heavy juggernauts chunky, lifesaving fire engines and "road trains." Road trains are a long-haul method in Australia; they transport goods across the outback. My friends say being a truck driver would be boring however, I disagree. Huge trucks are awe-inspiring driving one would be fantastic. Many long-haul drivers equip their trucks with the following; sleeping bunks, hot plates, and small refrigerators. I'll become a truck driver one day just watch me. I'll write a book about my life on the road: **One Truck Driver's Adventures.**

The Apostrophe (')

Apostrophes are used to make the possessive forms of words and to form contractions. The following rules explain the main uses for apostrophes.

Using Apostrophes

1. Add an apostrophe and *s* to form the possessive of singular words and plurals not ending in *s*.

Incorrect   Sarahs' calculator, the bus' engine, Ms. Jones house, the childrens' snack

Correct   the dog**'s** tail, Sarah**'s** calculator, the bus**'s** engine, Ms. Jones**'s** house

the children**'s** snack, the geese**'s** pond

When the end of the word is pronounced "eez," add only an apostrophe.

Correct   Achilles' heel, Ramses' tomb
Awkward   Achilles's heel, Ramses's tomb

2. To form the possessive of plural nouns ending in *s*, add an apostrophe.

Incorrect   the dogs's tails, the busses drivers, the Jones' house
Correct   the dogs**'** tails, the girls**'** desks, the busses**'** drivers, the Joneses**'** house

3. Use an apostrophe to form the possessive of indefinite pronouns but *not* personal pronouns.

Incorrect   her's, hers'   it's   your's   someones'   nobodys' everybodies'

Correct   someone, someone**'s**   nobody, nobody**'s**
everyone, everyone**'s**   she, her, hers
you, your, yours   they, their
it, its

4. Use an apostrophe in a contraction in place of the missing letter or letters.

Examples   cannot, can**'t**   he would, he**'d**   let us, let**'s**
it is, it**'s**   you are, you**'re**

Use Apostrophes to Form Possessives
Write the possessive form of each word in parentheses. The first item is completed for you.

1. the ____radio's____ volume (*radio*)

2. five _____ textbooks (*students*)

3. _____ favorite *(everybody)*

4. the _____ manager *(team)*

5. _____ skateboard *(Luke)*

6. several _____ nests *(birds)*

7. the _____ wrappers *(candies)*

8. _____ violin *(he)*

9. _____ labors *(Hercules)*

10. the _____ teacher *(class)*

Use Apostrophes to Form Contractions

Write the contraction of each of the following pairs of words. The first item is completed for you.

11. you are   _____*you're*_____

12. they are   _____

13. we would   _____

14. should not   _____

15. it is   _____

16. will not   _____

17. cannot   _____

18. I am   _____

19. we are   _____

20. could not   _____

Parentheses ( )

Parentheses are used to set off nonessential information from a sentence. The following rule explains the main use for parentheses.

Use parentheses to set off nonessential information added to a sentence.

Usually, the information is added to clarify an idea in the sentence and would make the sentence incorrect grammatically if it weren't enclosed in parentheses.

Incorrect	The Great Lakes there are five of them form the largest area of fresh water on earth.
Incorrect	The Great Lakes, there are five of them, form the largest area of fresh water on earth.
Correct	The Great Lakes **(**there are five of them**)** form the largest area of fresh water on earth.
Incorrect	Robert Frost 1874–1963 wrote many of America's best-loved poems.
Correct	Robert Frost **(**1874–1963**)** wrote many of America's best-loved poems.

Use Parentheses Correctly

Add parentheses where they are needed in each sentence below.

| Example | By the time I walked home *(it took forty-five minutes)*, dinner was cold and Mom was worried. |

1. The Pacific Ocean it lies to America's west is the world's largest ocean.

2. Not just a scientist, Benjamin Franklin 1706–1790 was also a printer, an inventor, and a diplomat.

3. As a child I always loved visits to Aunt Henrietta my dad's sister and her large family.

4. Did you know the color of clouds white or gray is due to their moisture content?

5. Please go get my sketchbook the one with the brown cover and a handful of colored pencils.

Quotation Marks (" ")

Use quotation marks to enclose direct quotations and dialogue.
Direct quotations are someone else's exact words, whether written or spoken. *Dialogue* is conversation such as you see written in short stories and novels.

| Incorrect | He said, If you make a home run, we'll win the game. |
| Correct | He said, **"**If you make a home run, we'll win the game.**"** |

Quotation marks enclose only the person's exact words, not expressions like *he said*.

Incorrect   "If you make a home run, he said, we'll win the game."
Correct   **"**If you make a home run,**"** he said, **"**we'll win the game.**"**

Place a comma after expressions like *he said* when they introduce a quotation.

Incorrect   She said "We are sure to be victorious."
Correct   She said**,** "We are sure to be victorious.**"**

Place a period or comma following a quotation inside the quotation marks.

Incorrect   I replied, "Yes, but the game isn't over yet".
Correct   I replied, "Yes, but the game isn't over yet**."**

Incorrect   "Yes", I replied, "but the game isn't over yet."
Correct   "Yes**,"** I replied, "but the game isn't over yet."

Place a semicolon or colon outside quotation marks. Place a question mark or exclamation point inside the quotation marks if it is part of the quote.

Incorrect   Someone mentioned "the dynamics of competition;" I didn't understand him.
Correct   Someone mentioned "the dynamics of competition**";** I didn't understand him.

Incorrect   Haj asked, "Who is the other team's pitcher"?
Correct   Haj asked, "Who is the other team's pitcher**?"** *(The quoted words ask a question, so the question mark goes **inside** the quotation marks.)*

Incorrect   What is the meaning of the phrase "dynamics of competition?"
Correct   What is the meaning of the phrase "dynamics of competition**"?** *(The quoted words are not a question, so the question mark goes **outside** the quotation marks.)*

Use Quotation Marks Correctly

Insert quotation marks where they are needed in the following sentences. Use a carat (∧) to indicate exact placement in tight spots. The first item is completed for you.

1. Who wrote the story about the "notorious jumping frog?**"**∧

2. Freddie said, I've been hearing strange noises at night.

3. There are five minutes left in the exam period, said Ms. Ewing.

4. Someone shouted, Watch out!

5. Who shouted Watch out!?

6. Leaving the cinema, I said, It's too bad I wasted seven dollars on that ticket.

7. Are you a fan of Louis Armstrong's jazz music? he asked.

8. When you come over, Julia said, we'll order pizza.

9. The poet wrote of hills of white velvet: clouds.

10. Trey said, I'll help you with your science project; then he added, unless Ben is helping you.

Multiple Choice

Choose the best way to punctuate each underlined word group. If no change is best, choose NO CHANGE.

Mark <u>Twain pen name of Samuel Clemens</u> is
                        1

the author of **The Adventures of Tom Sawyer.** The

_____ **1.** **A.** NO CHANGE
   B. Twain; pen name of Samuel Clemens,
   C. Twain: pen name of Samuel Clemens
   D. Twain (pen name of Samuel Clemens)

<u>tales characters</u> <u>include</u> Tom <u>Sawyer Huckleberry Finn</u>
        2   3   4

<u>and Aunt Sally</u>.
        4

_____ **2.** **A.** NO CHANGE
   B. tale's characters
   C. tales' characters
   D. tales's characters

_____ **3.** **A.** NO CHANGE
   B. include: Tom
   C. include, Tom
   D. include; Tom

_____ **4.** **A.** NO CHANGE
   B. Sawyer; Huckleberry Finn; and Aunt Sally
   C. Sawyer, Huckleberry Finn, and Aunt Sally
   D. Sawyer, Huckleberry Finn and, Aunt Sally

In one of the most well-known <u>scenes; Tom</u> is given
₅

_____ 5. A. NO CHANGE
     B. scenes: Tom
     C. scenes Tom
     D. scenes, Tom

the chore of <u>whitewashing painting</u> a fence. He <u>doesnt</u>
₆   ₇

_____ 6. A. NO CHANGE
     B. whitewashing: painting
     C. whitewashing (painting)
     D. whitewashing "painting"

_____ 7. A. NO CHANGE
     B. doesn't
     C. does'nt
     D. doesnt'

want to do the <u>work and, he</u> devises a clever plan. He
₈

pretends to have a fantastic time painting the fence.

_____ 8. A. NO CHANGE
     B. work; and he
     C. work and he
     D. work, and he

When another boy sees him having <u>fun, that</u> boy wants
₉

_____ 9. A. NO CHANGE
     B. fun that
     C. fun! that
     D. fun; that

to paint. Other boys come <u>along after a while</u> Tom is
₁₀

relaxing while others do the chore for him.

_____ 10. A. NO CHANGE
      B. along, after a while,
      C. along; after a while,
      D. along after a while,

Twain is known for <u>his</u> <u>humorous enjoyable tales</u>
₁₁   ₁₂

_____ 11. A. NO CHANGE
      B. he's
      C. his'
      D. he

_____ 12. A. NO CHANGE
      B. humorous, enjoy-able, tales
      C. humorous "enjoy-able" tales
      D. humorous, enjoy-able tales

for his <u>stories</u> portrayal of the South. In an essay on
13

_____ 13. **A.** NO CHANGE
  B. stories'
  C. story's
  D. stories's

writing, Twain <u>wrote The</u> difference between the almost
14

right word and the right word is really a large matter—

_____ 14. **A.** NO CHANGE
  B. wrote, "The
  C. wrote "The
  D. wrote, The

'tis the difference between the lightning-bug and

<u>lightning</u>
15

_____ 15. **A.** NO CHANGE
  B. lightning".
  C. lightning."
  D. lightning"!

Short Answer

Use the checklist to answer the following question.

Writer's Checklist

✓ Using End Marks
✓ Using Commas
✓ Using Apostrophes
✓ Using Parentheses

"Watch out," yelled Joseph as the books came crashing down from the shelf near Kyles head.

You have been asked by a fellow student to peer edit the above sentence. Using the checklist, give the writer feedback by identifying the two rules that apply to the punctuation errors in the sentence. Then rewrite the sentence correctly.

_____

_____

_____

_____

_____

_____

_____

Look & Learn

Imagine that you have never seen the written English language before. To you, English letters look like squiggles. Now look at the following lines of text:

"A newspaper is a collection of half-injustices," wrote Stephen Crane.

As you scan the lines of "printed squiggles," which ones stand out? Your eye probably lingered on the markings that seemed different from the rest—perhaps the punctuation, but definitely the capital letters. Capital letters are bigger than other letters, and they grab the eye's attention whether you understand the language or not. In the lines of text above, the words *A, Stephen,* and *Crane* stand out because they begin with capital letters.

In the Spotlight

Why Capitalize?

English uses capital letters to set apart a word from surrounding words. The reasons to do so are varied. For example, a capital letter helps mark the beginning of a sentence, and it helps set proper nouns apart from common nouns. In this lesson, you will review these and other reasons for using capital letters as well as guidelines for using capitalization correctly.

The main rules for capitalization are as follows.

1. Capitalize the first word in a sentence.

Examples   **P**lease hand me that dictionary.

How do you spell *miniature*?

2. Capitalize the first word in a quotation if the quotation is a complete sentence.

Examples   Anthony said, "**W**hen I got there, the race was over."

"**W**hen I got there," Anthony said, "the race was over." (The word <u>the</u> in the second part of the quotation is not capitalized because it continues the complete sentence begun with <u>When</u>.)

Written dialogue often contains incomplete sentences that stand alone like sentences. In written dialogue, capitalize the first word in a word or word group set as a sentence.

Incorrect	He said, "ready to go?"
	I shrugged. "sure."
Correct	He said, "**R**eady to go?"
	I shrugged. "**S**ure."

3. Capitalize the pronoun *I*.

| Incorrect | Joe, Hester, and i laughed. |
| Correct | Joe, Hester, and **I** laughed. |

Use Capitalization Correctly

The following passage is taken from Herman Melville's story "Bartleby, the Scrivener." Bartleby is a copyist in a law office, and in this excerpt his boss calls him to help proofread some papers he copied out by hand.

Correct errors in capitalization in the passage. Cross out each lowercase letter that should be capitalized and write the capital above it. Cross out capital letters that should be lowercase and write the lowercase above. There are ten errors. The first error is corrected for you.

> $\overset{Q}{}$
> "Bartleby! ~~q~~uick, i am waiting."
>
> I heard a slow scrape of his chair legs on the uncarpeted floor, and
>
> Soon he appeared standing at the entrance of his hermitage.
>
> "what is wanted?" Said he mildly.
>
> "the copies, the copies" said i hurriedly. "we are going to examine
>
> them. there"—and I held towards him the fourth quadruplicate.
>
> "I would prefer not to," He said, and gently disappeared behind the
>
> screen.

4. Capitalize proper nouns.

Proper nouns include the specific names of people, places, things, events, and times.

| People | **T**oni **M**orrison, **M**s. **R**uiz, Uncle **T**om, **G**overnor **T**aft, **P**rincipal **C**arver |
| Places | **Y**ellowstone **N**ational **P**ark, **D**ayton, **A**rctic **C**ircle, **A**laska, **Y**ale **U**niversity |

Things	**B**rooklyn **B**ridge, **F**rench, *Titanic,* **S**tatue of **L**iberty, **H**oover **D**am
Events	**A**merican **R**evolution, **H**urricane **H**ugo, **S**cholastic **B**ook **F**air
Times	**R**enaissance, **S**tone **A**ge, **T**hursday, **O**ctober, **M**emorial **D**ay

Do not capitalize words such as *uncle, park,* and *university* if they are not part of a specific name.

Incorrect	my Uncle, strict Principal, pretty Park, that University, bloody Revolution
Correct	my **u**ncle, strict **p**rincipal, pretty **p**ark, that **u**niversity, bloody **r**evolution

5. Capitalize proper adjectives.
Proper adjectives are formed from proper nouns.

Examples	**S**panish tile, **G**reek architecture, **C**anadian citizen, **I**talian peninsula

6. Capitalize titles.
Capitalize the first, last, and main words of a title. Do not capitalize *a, an, the,* and short prepositions such as *of* (unless they are the first word of a title or sentence).

Books	*The Red Badge of Courage, A Wrinkle in Time, To Kill a Mockingbird*
Articles	"How to Fix a Flat Tire," "Five Teen Hangouts," "Fire Injures Seven"
Stories	"A White Heron," "The Fall of the House of Usher," "Man in Hiding"
Poems	"Mending Wall," "Prairie Waters by Night," "Refugee in America"

Revise Sentences to Correct Errors in Capitalization
Rewrite each sentence, capitalizing it correctly. If the sentence is already correct, write *no change.*

Example	When my Sister, ginger, goes to College next Fall, I'll finally have my own room.

When my sister, Ginger, goes to college next fall, I'll finally have my own room.

1. Have you read the novel *dandelion wine* by ray bradbury?

_____

2. "The brazilian rain forest is fascinating," my grandmother said.

_____

3. At the library, I requested help finding "The black cat" by edgar allan poe.

_____

4. In this museum, you'll find artifacts from Roman ruins.

_____

5. "I'll meet you at the riverview mall on friday night," Aunt Leah said.

_____

On Your Own

In each numbered item below, identify the word or word group containing a capitalization error. If the item is already correct, choose *No error.*

_____ **1.** the word *graffiti*, used often by English speakers, is actually an
       A   **B**   **C**

       Italian word. No error
       D   **E**

_____ **2.** Hattie woke me early on Saturday and said, "Let's wash the car." I
       A   **B**   **C**

       replied, "no thanks." No error
           D   **E**

_____ **3.** You and I will do our project on the Great Depression, which oc-
         A   **B**   **C**

       curred in the United States during the 1930s. No error
              D   **E**

_____ **4.** My great-grandfather told me stories of his boyhood in Oklahoma
           A   **B**   **C**

       during the dust bowl in the 1930s. No error
            D   **E**

_____ **5.** The tearful student turned to professor McGrorty and said, "Why
       A   **B**   **C**

       did I flunk the history test?" No error
              D   **E**

_____ **6.** *Gods and generals*, written by Jeff M. Shaara, is the story of four
       A   **B**

       generals in the Civil War. No error
       C   **D**   **E**

_____ 7. After crossing the <u>Golden Gate Bridge</u>, the <u>mayor</u> entered
A **B**

San <u>francisco</u> and drove toward the <u>city's</u> downtown area. <u>No error</u>
C **D** **E**

_____ 8. Every evening <u>Mom</u> asks me what I did in <u>school</u> that day. <u>I</u> always
A **B** **C**

say, "<u>Nothing</u>." <u>No error</u>
D **E**

_____ 9. Due to <u>global warming</u>, glaciers around the <u>world</u> are slowly melting.
A **B**

<u>dangerous</u> floods and damaged <u>river</u> levees could result. <u>No error</u>
C **D** **E**

_____ 10. The _<u>Mars odyssey</u>_, <u>which</u> orbited <u>Mars</u> in early 2002, located large
A **B** **C**

amounts of frozen water buried at the <u>planet's</u> south pole. <u>No error</u>
D **E**

_____ 11. Where would you rather go for a vacation: the <u>Grand Canyon</u>,
A

Australia's <u>great barrier reef</u>, the <u>Florida coast</u>, or a <u>water park</u> in a
B **C** **D**

nearby city? <u>No error</u>
E

_____ 12. The <u>Gettysburg Address</u>, delivered by <u>President</u> Abraham Lincoln
A **B**

on <u>November</u> 19, 1863, is one of our <u>nation's</u> most famous speeches.
C **D**

<u>No error</u>
E

_____ 13. At a <u>bookstore</u>, I found _<u>Bronx Masquerade</u>_ by <u>nikki grimes</u>, who
A **B** **C**

won the 2003 <u>Coretta Scott King Award</u> for the book. <u>No error</u>
D **E**

_____ 14. My <u>aunt's</u> recipe for brownies calls for <u>dutch chocolate</u>, fresh <u>farm</u>
A **B** **C**

eggs, real <u>creamery</u> butter, and (of course) sugar. <u>No error</u>
D **E**

_____ 15. In their study of the <u>dark ages</u>, the students learned that the <u>age</u>
A **B**

began with the fall of <u>Rome</u> in the late fifth <u>century</u> and continued
C **D**

to about A.D. 1000. <u>No error</u>
E

Lesson 2 OGT Practice: Spelling, Punctuation, and Capitalization

Multiple Choice

Instructions: Certain words and phrases in the following passage are underlined and numbered. In the right-hand column, you will find alternatives for each underlined part. Choose the alternative showing the best way to revise and improve the selection. If the original version is best, choose NO CHANGE.

The first Friday night after school let out for the

summer, the three of us met at <u>Movies Eight.</u> It stood on
1

    1. **A.** NO CHANGE
            B. Movies Eight,
            C. movies eight.
            D. Moveis Eight.

the busiest corner in <u>town Hines</u> Boulevard and Park
2

    2. **A.** NO CHANGE
            B. town; Hines
            C. town: Hines
            D. town, hines

<u>Street; As</u> Quinn and Trent piled out of their taxi cab, I
3

stared up at the brilliantly lit marquee. Which movie

did I want to see?

    3. **A.** NO CHANGE
            B. street; as
            C. Street. as
            D. Street. As

    "<u>Lets see</u> the romantic comedy," said Quinn. "I love
4

    4. **A.** NO CHANGE
            B. "lets see
            C. Let's see
            D. "Let's see

<u>comedys.</u>" Opening her handbag, she dug through the
5

    5. **A.** NO CHANGE
            B. comedies
            C. comedeys
            D. comedis

lip balm, <u>mints tissues and keys</u> to find her wallet.
6

    6. **A.** NO CHANGE
            B. mints, tissues and, keys
            C. mints, tissues, and keys
            D. mints tissues, and keys

"No" said Trent, _"I want to see the sci-fi adventure"_
7   8

_____ **7. A.** NO CHANGE
          B. "No," said
          C. "No." said
          D. "No" said

_____ **8. A.** NO CHANGE
          B. Adventure."
          C. adventure".
          D. adventure."

Smiling, I _said, "then_ I'm the tie-breaker. Sci-fi
            9

_____ **9. A.** NO CHANGE
          B. said "then
          C. said, "Then
          D. said: "Then

adventure, here we _come!"_
         10

_____ **10. A.** NO CHANGE
          B. come"!
          C. come".
          D. come!

Short Answer
Use the checklist to answer the following question.

Writer's Checklist

✓ Spelling
✓ Capitalization
✓ Punctuation

In William Shakespeare's _Romeo and Juliet_, Juliet's family (the capulets) wanted her to marry Paris, however, she had already given her heart to Romeo.

You have been asked by a fellow student to peer edit the above sentence. Using the checklist, give the writer feedback by identifying the two rules that apply to the errors in the sentence. Then rewrite the sentence correctly.

_____

_____

_____

_____

_____

_____

_____

Lesson 3 Using Grammar

Writing Conventions Benchmark

C. Demonstrate understanding of the grammatical conventions of the English language.

"What's the big deal about using correct grammar?" you may ask. "I always get my point across, even if I do make mistakes."

But do you always get your point across? Or do grammar mistakes make your reader understand one thing while you *think* you said something else? Consider the following example:

Built of white limestone, Fritz studied the building.

Thanks to a grammar mistake, this sentence says that Fritz is built of white limestone. (The phrase *Built of white limestone* modifies *Fritz.*) Certainly the writer didn't mean to say this, but it is what the reader may understand. What the writer meant to say is

Fritz studied the building built of white limestone.

Unfortunately, you cannot follow your writing around, telling readers "What I meant to say is . . ." Your writing must speak for itself. Correct grammar helps avoid confusion and misunderstanding, and it gives your writing power. Not only that, but correct grammar is a sign of good education and careful thinking, commanding credibility and respect.

The OGT Writing will test your ability to recognize and correct errors in grammar through a variety of multiple-choice questions. Many grammar and usage rules will be familiar to you, either because you have learned them or because you follow them in your everyday speech and writing. Lesson 3 provides review and practice in six aspects of grammar that form the focus of OGT grammar questions:

parts of speech
verb tenses
clauses
phrases
modifiers
parallel structure

As with spelling, punctuation, and capitalization, mastering grammar requires review and lots of practice. Take charge of your learning process by going through the lessons as often as you need to and asking questions whenever something is unclear. Practice what you've learned by using grammar correctly, not only as you prepare for the OGT but in other classes and situations as well. Good luck in your studies!

Look & Learn

Recall a conversation that you had recently with a friend. What did you talk about? Did you make plans to study, play ball, or get together later? Did you argue? Or make up after a fight? Now imagine trying to express the same ideas without using verbs. A simple conversation about lunch would sound a lot like toddlers speaking.

"I hungry."
"Me too. Where food?"

When it comes to expressing ideas, verbs are the core of a sentence. They express the action or state of being that the sentence is about. They help us make our ideas clear, and they indicate the time (past, present, or future) that we are talking about. Every complete sentence has a verb or verb phrase.

In the Spotlight

The Verb

The *verb* is one of the eight parts of speech. Its job is to express action or to link the subject to another word in the sentence.

Action verb   Leona **studied**. (Studied expresses an action Leona performed.)

Linking verb   She **felt** confident. (Felt links She to confident.)

Action verbs and *linking verbs* are the two types of main verbs. These main verbs may receive help from *helping verbs*.

Helping verb   Leona **had** studied. (Had helps the action verb studied.)

She **was** feeling confident. (Was helps the linking verb feeling.)

Helping verbs include the "being verbs" *am, is, are, was, were, be, being,* and *been,* as well as *have, has, had, do, does, did, will, should, would, may, might, must, can,* and *could.*

Together, the main verb and its helping verb(s) form a verb phrase.

Verb phrase   Leona **had studied**.

She **has been feeling** confident.

To prepare for the OGT Writing, learn to identify verb phrases, including *action*, *linking*, and *helping* verbs. This will help you to identify and correct errors in the use of *verb tense* on the test.

The **tense** of a verb expresses when the action takes place—in the past, present, or future. Tense also indicates whether the action is completed or is ongoing. Even though you will not have to label verbs on the OGT, understanding verbs and verb phrases is necessary in order to decide the tense.

English has six basic verb tenses: present, past, future, present perfect, past perfect, and future perfect. These forms are illustrated in the table below.

Basic Forms of the Six Verb Tenses

Present Tense	expresses action in the present or action that habitually happens She **walks** all over town.
Past Tense	expresses action that happened sometime in the past She **walked** to a park yesterday.
Future Tense	expresses action that will happen at some future time She **will walk** to a soccer game tomorrow.
Present Perfect	expresses action that is completed in the present She **has walked** to Hannah's house.
Past Perfect	expresses action that was completed at a definite time in the past She **had walked** around the lake before dawn yesterday.
Future Perfect	expresses action that will be completed at a definite time in the future She **will have walked** to six friends' houses by this weekend.

Notice that helping verbs are used to express many tenses. In fact, by looking at the helping verb, you often can identify the verb tense. Try it out. What are the verb tenses in these two sentences?

Amanda can drive the car.

Amanda did drive the car.

Even though the verb phrases use the same main verb *(drive)*, each uses a different helping verb. In the first sentence, the helping verb *can* indicates present tense. In the second sentence, *did* indicates past tense.

Verbs are often modified by adverbs, which are another part of speech. However, an adverb never affects the verb tense. In each example below, the verb is <u>underlined</u>, and the adverb is printed in **bold.**

Chad <u>will have called</u> me by Tuesday. *(no adverb)*

Chad <u>will</u> **not** <u>have called</u> me by Tuesday. *(Adverb interrupts verb phrase.)*

Chad **definitely** <u>will have called</u> me by Tuesday. *(adverb before verb phrase)*

In each example, the verb tense is the same: future perfect. The action will have been completed by a certain time in the future.

Sometimes, part of a verb phrase is in a contraction, such as *he'd* (he would) and *they'll* (they will). To decide the verb tense, take the helping verb from the contraction and examine it along with the rest of the verb.

<u>I'</u>ll write you often. (<u>I'</u>ll contains part of the verb phrase.)

I <u>will write</u> you often.

By recognizing *will* as part of the verb phrase, you are able to identify the verb tense as future tense. However, if you overlook *will* and focus only on *write,* the tense seems to be present tense.

In the following exercise, practice identifying verb tenses. Watch carefully for contractions and adverbs. If it's helpful, cross out adverbs and break apart contractions, writing the separate words above the contractions.

Identify Verbs and Verb Tenses

For each sentence, write the verb or verb phrase. Then identify the verb tense: *past, present, future, past perfect, present perfect,* or *future perfect.*

Example   Before dinnertime, I will have taught Scruffy a new trick.

will have taught—future perfect

1. Finally the train chugged around the snowy mountain.

2. My math and history homework will be complete by eight o'clock.

3. I don't care about the set decoration at this early point.

4. He has applied for a card at a nearby branch of the library.

5. Despite the heat, the family reunion picnic was a success.

6. After school, Carrie will drive me to Megan's house.

_____

7. Paulo had noticed the football playbook on the bench.

_____

8. With this bone, the dog will have buried a dozen in the yard.

_____

9. Before school, I'll jog a mile.

_____

10. Alfred and Wes have already practiced their duet.

_____

Each basic verb tense also has a *progressive* form, which shows continuous or ongoing action.

Progressive Forms of the Six Verb Tenses

Present Progressive	expresses action that is ongoing right now She **is walking** to the corner market.
Past Progressive	expresses action that was ongoing in the past She **was walking** around town yesterday.
Future Progressive	expresses action that will be ongoing at some future time She **will be walking** again soon.
Present Perfect Progressive	expresses ongoing action completed in the present She **has been walking** everywhere for years.
Past Perfect Progressive	expresses ongoing action completed in the past She **had been walking** to Trent's house before he moved.
Future Perfect Progressive	expresses ongoing action to be completed in the future She **will have been walking** the river trail for a year on Friday.

To identify progressive verb forms, remember these tips:

- The *-ing* ending of the main verb signals the progressive tense.
- The first verb in the verb phrase indicates present, past, or future action.
- The helping verb *been* indicates a perfect tense.

Identify Progressive Verb Forms

Read each sentence and decide the verb's tense. Then write the letter of the verb tense on the line next to the sentence. Use each tense only once. Item 1 is completed for you.

(a) present progressive   (d) present perfect progressive
(b) past progressive   (e) past perfect progressive
(c) future progressive   (f) future perfect progressive

___f___   **1.** On his birthday, John will have been practicing guitar for a year.

_____   **2.** They were planning a surprise party for Ms. Howard.

_____   **3.** I have been thinking about that math problem.

_____   **4.** The Fritzes had been reading aloud as a family each evening.

_____   **5.** Next summer, Zelda will be working as a camp counselor.

_____   **6.** You are behaving strangely.

Principal Parts of Verbs

Verb tenses are based on the principal parts of verbs—that is, the different forms each verb can take. The four principal parts of verbs are *present* (or *base*) *form, present participle, past,* and *past participle.* When you list the principal parts of a verb, you are *conjugating* the verb. The table below shows the conjugations of *talk* and *sing.*

Four Principal Parts of Verbs

PRESENT	PRESENT PARTICIPLE	PAST	PAST PARTICIPLE
talk	talking	talked	(have) talked
sing	singing	sang	(have) sung

The past participle is always used with a helping verb. For this reason, the word *have* is included in parentheses to distinguish the past participle from the past form.

For all verbs, form the present participle by adding *-ing* to the present form.

| *Present* | kiss | giggle | eat | fall |
| *Present participle* | kiss**ing** | giggl**ing** | eat**ing** | fall**ing** |

However, verbs vary in the ways in which the past and past participle are formed. Depending on how these parts are formed, we categorize a verb as *regular* or *irregular*. The past and past participle of a **regular verb** are formed by adding *-d* or *-ed* to the present form. The table below shows the conjugation of regular verbs. Most verbs are regular.

Regular Verbs

PRESENT	PRESENT PARTICIPLE	PAST	PAST PARTICIPLE
kiss	kissing	kissed	(have) kissed
giggle	giggling	giggled	(have) giggled
practice	practicing	practiced	(have) practiced
want	wanting	wanted	(have) wanted
call	calling	called	(have) called

Conjugate Regular Verbs

Fill in the table by writing the correct forms of each verb. The first item is completed for you.

PRESENT	PRESENT PARTICIPLE	PAST	PAST PARTICIPLE
1. kick	kicking	_kicked_	(have) _kicked_
2. march	_____	marched	(have) _____
3. paint	_____	_____	(have) painted
4. play	playing	_____	(have) _____
5. remember	_____	remembered	(have) _____
6. trade	trading	_____	(have) _____

But what happens when you try to add *-ed* to *eat*? Or to *fall*? *Eated* and *falled* are not proper words. These verbs, like many others, are **irregular verbs**. Their past and past participle are formed some other way than by adding *-d* or *-ed* to the present form. The following table shows the conjugation of some commonly used irregular verbs.

Irregular Verbs

PRESENT	PRESENT PARTICIPLE	PAST	PAST PARTICIPLE
become	becoming	became	(have) become
begin	beginning	began	(have) begun
bring	bringing	brought	(have) brought
choose	choosing	chose	(have) chosen
dive	diving	dove *or* dived	(have) dived
do	doing	did	(have) done
drink	drinking	drank	(have) drunk
eat	eating	ate	(have) eaten
fall	falling	fell	(have) fallen
fly	flying	flown	(have) flown
get	getting	got	(have) got *or* gotten
have	having	had	(have) had
hear	hearing	heard	(have) heard
hide	hiding	hid	(have) hidden *or* hid
light	lighting	lighted *or* lit	(have) lighted *or* lit
lose	losing	lost	(have) lost
ride	riding	rode	(have) ridden
ring	ringing	rang	(have) rung
say	saying	said	(have) said
see	seeing	saw	(have) seen
sink	sinking	sank *or* sunk	(have) sunk
speak	speaking	spoke	(have) spoken
swim	swimming	swam	(have) swum
take	taking	took	(have) taken
throw	throwing	threw	(have) thrown
write	writing	wrote	(have) written

As you study for the OGT, whenever you are unsure of the conjugation of a verb, grab a dictionary. The entry for the present form of an irregular verb shows its conjugation (sometimes labeled "inflected forms"). If you find yourself looking up the same words repeatedly, make a study sheet. Then study these verbs in the way that works best for you. Some students learn well through memorization, while others learn better by writing out the conjugation over and over. Others would rather write sentences using each form of the verb in its proper context. Perhaps a mixture of these techniques appeals to you.

When you take the OGT Writing, you will *not* have access to a dictionary. For this reason, your study and practice ahead of time are crucial to mastering the OGT.

Conjugate Irregular Verbs

Fill in the table by writing the correct forms of each verb. The first item is completed for you.

PRESENT	PRESENT PARTICIPLE	PAST	PAST PARTICIPLE
1. choose	choosing	_chose_	(have) _chosen_
2. fall	falling	_____	(have) _____
3. ride	_____	rode	(have) _____
4. _____	throwing	_____	(have) thrown
5. begin	beginning	_____	(have) _____
6. speak	_____	_____	(have) spoken

Use a Dictionary to Conjugate Irregular Verbs

Use a dictionary to learn the conjugations of each of these irregular verbs. Write each conjugation on the lines provided. The first item is completed for you.

PRESENT	PRESENT PARTICIPLE	PAST	PAST PARTICIPLE
7. find	_finding_	_found_	(have) _found_
8. cost	_____	_____	(have) _____
9. hit	_____	_____	(have) _____
10. draw	_____	_____	(have) _____
11. spend	_____	_____	(have) _____
12. stand	_____	_____	(have) _____

Use Correct Forms of Irregular Verbs

Underline the correct form of each verb in parentheses.

Example   Police learned that the thief had (*get*, *gotten*) into the apartment by using the fire escape.

13. A spare house key was *(hide, hided, hidden)* under the doormat.

14. The captains have *(chose, chosen, choosed)* their team members.

15. When the alarm *(rang, ringed, rung),* I awoke.

16. During the long bus ride, I was glad I had *(brang, brought, brung)* a snack.

17. I *(saw, seen, sawed)* what happened.

Consistent Verb Tense

So far in Lesson 3.1, you have learned about two main topics: verb tense and verb conjugation. Now, with this knowledge, you have a new skill available to you: maintaining the use of appropriate verb tense.

Verbs in a sentence or passage should express a logical, correct sequence of time. Events that happen at the same time should be expressed in the same tense. The examples below show consistent use of verb tense. (Remember that in a verb phrase, the first verb in the phrase indicates the tense.)

Examples   Emily Dickinson <u>wrote</u> hundreds of poems. However, she
                past

                <u>did</u> not give them titles.
                past

                Adrienne Rich <u>has</u> written many poems. She <u>has</u> often
                                      present   *present*
                chosen love as a theme.

Sometimes different tenses are used in the same sentence or passage to express actions that happened at different times.

Examples   I <u>am</u> reading *A Separate Peace*. John Knowles <u>wrote</u> it. *(I*
          present   *past*
          am reading a book [present tense] that is already written

          [past tense].)

          Lucas <u>looked</u> for a copy of *To Kill a Mockingbird*. He
               past

          <u>will</u> be reading it in English class. *(Lucas already looked*
          future
          for the book [past tense] that he will read later [future

          tense].)

Errors in the use of verb tense occur when a writer changes, or shifts, from one tense to another without logic. This is called a faulty shift in tense.

Incorrect	Aviva <u>turned</u> to the last act of *Romeo and Juliet* and <u>cries</u> *past* *present* at the ending. *(It seems the sentence is about something that happened in the past. But the tense shifts from past to present)*
Correct	Aviva <u>turned</u> to the last act of *Romeo and Juliet* and <u>cried</u> *past* *past* at the ending.
Incorrect	As I <u>was</u> staring at the stacks of books, the librarian *past* <u>offers</u> assistance. *(The sentence begins with ongoing* *present* *action in the past, but it makes a faulty shift to the present.)*

Correct	As I <u>was</u> staring at the stacks of books, the librarian
	      past
	 <u>offered</u> assistance.
	    past

Incorrect	Each weekend Ryan <u>reads</u> a whole novel. He <u>enjoyed</u> this *present* *past* time alone. *(These events happen at the same time. The time may be present, or it may be past.)*
Correct	Each weekend Ryan <u>reads</u> a whole novel. He <u>enjoys</u> this *present* *present* time alone.
Correct	Each weekend Ryan <u>read</u> a whole novel. He <u>enjoyed</u> this *past* *past* time alone.

On the OGT, you may be asked to recognize faulty tense shifts and choose the best correction. The first exercise below gives you practice in recognizing faulty tense shifts. The second exercise asks you to recognize faulty shifts and choose the best corrections for them.

Identify Faulty Shifts in Verb Tense

The verbs and verb phrases in each item are underlined. Decide whether each item has a faulty tense shift or needs no change. On the line, write *faulty shift* or *no change*.

Example   <u>   *faulty shift*   </u> When I <u>learn</u> something new in

school, I <u>related</u> it to my own life.

_____ **1.** Whenever I <u>am watching</u> television, I <u>was</u> on guard against propaganda.

_____ **2.** Last week in English class, we <u>studied</u> propaganda. This persuasive technique <u>is</u> a deliberate attempt to "sell" people a belief or product.

_____ **3.** By "sell," I <u>mean</u> "persuade to purchase, believe, or support." Propaganda <u>will use</u> these techniques.

_____ **4.** I <u>saw</u> one television commercial about teen skin care products. It <u>portrays</u> a person with one blemish as totally unattractive.

_____ **5.** One or two blemishes <u>do</u> not <u>make</u> you unattractive. However, companies <u>sell</u> this idea of unattractiveness. As a result, they <u>sell</u> more products.

Use Verb Tense Correctly

Choose the best correction for each underlined word or word group. If the sentence is correct, choose NO CHANGE.

Example   Now I believe many propaganda messages (though not all of them) <u>will be</u> the same as lies.

  A. NO CHANGE

  B. are being

  C. are

  D. will have been

6. After I studied the concept of propaganda in school, I <u>look</u> for it all around me.

  A. NO CHANGE

  B. will look

  C. was looking

  D. looked

7. Now I see it everywhere. It is in television commercials, of course. It <u>will also be</u> in music videos, print advertisements, and newspapers.

  A. NO CHANGE

  B. was also

  C. is also

  D. also will be

8. For me, peer pressure <u>has been</u> a kind of propaganda. It has directed my choice in clothes, in music, and in personal opinions.

  A. NO CHANGE

  B. was

    C. will be

    D. had been

9. Survey results <u>were</u> propaganda as well. The survey itself often fits a particular purpose of the pollster.

    A. NO CHANGE

    B. have been

    C. can be

    D. will have been

10. A survey says, "Four out of five dentists recommend this tooth-brush!" The same dentists may recommend other toothbrushes too. But the pollsters <u>were not mentioning</u> that part of the results.

    A. NO CHANGE

    B. don't mention

    C. weren't mentioning

    D. didn't mention

 Choose the best correction for each underlined word or word group. If it is correct as is, choose NO CHANGE.

A God, a Fish, and a Jaguar

When an earthquake occurs, the earth shakes,

vibrates, and sometimes <u>is cracking</u>. Buildings
             1

      ____ **1. A.** NO CHANGE
             B. cracks
             C. cracked
             D. will crack

<u>crumbled</u> and bridges may collapse, especially as a
 2

      ____ **2. A.** NO CHANGE
             B. crumbled
             C. crumbling
             D. may crumble

result of strong tremors. Nowadays, earthquakes

are no mystery. Scientists have studied them and <u>wrote</u>
                                    3

      ____ **3. A.** NO CHANGE
             B. are writing
             C. have written
             D. have wrote

countless books and articles about them.

But this abundance of knowledge <u>has not always</u>
                                  4

      ____ **4. A.** NO CHANGE
             B. has been
             C. will not always be
             D. is not always

<u>been</u> the case. The ancient Greeks, for example,
 4

<u>devise</u> a nonscientific explanation. They believed an
5

     5. **A.** NO CHANGE
          B. will devise
          C. were devising
          D. devised

earthquake occurred when Atlas <u>shrugs</u>. (Atlas, they
6

     6. **A.** NO CHANGE
          B. is shrugging
          C. shrugged
          D. will shrug

believed, was the god who <u>will carry</u> the world on
7

his shoulders.) According to an ancient Japanese

explanation, an enormous catfish

     7. **A.** NO CHANGE
          B. carried
          C. has been carrying
          D. is carrying

lived inside the earth. When it <u>is moving</u> around, the
8

earth trembled. Across the world in Mexico, ancient

     8. **A.** NO CHANGE
          B. moved
          C. moves
          D. has been moving

people <u>decided</u> earthquakes happened when a
9

     9. **A.** NO CHANGE
          B. decide
          C. were deciding
          D. had been deciding

powerful jaguar <u>bumps</u> against the pillars holding
10

up the world.

     10. **A.** NO CHANGE
          B. has bumped
          C. will bump
          D. bumped

& Learn

You do it automatically, every time you speak. You pull together a collection of clauses to form sentences that express your thoughts. Rarely, if ever, do you think, "Let's see, I need a main clause in every sentence, and I need to join every subordinate clause to a main clause." Instead, you just speak.

Of course, writing down these clauses to form complete sentences is more of a challenge. How do the different clauses fit together correctly? Which ones can stand alone as sentences? How do you recognize a subordinate clause?

This lesson reviews clauses and their functions. You'll get practice recognizing clauses and putting them together to form correct sentences. You'll also get practice correcting paragraphs that use clauses incorrectly.

In the Spotlight

The Clause

A *clause* is a word group containing a subject and its verb.

Example 1   I tossed a penny into the fountain.
Example 2   after I fed the pigeons

A *main clause* expresses a complete thought and can stand alone as a sentence. Example 1 above is a main clause.

A *subordinate clause* does not express a complete thought and cannot stand alone as a sentence. Example 2 above is a subordinate clause.

You can mix and match clauses to form sentences.

Example   After I fed the pigeons, I tossed a penny into the fountain.

The OGT Writing will test your ability to use clauses correctly. You should know how to

• tell whether a clause is main or subordinate

• identify the error of a subordinate clause standing alone

• join subordinate clauses to main clauses to form complete sentences

This lesson will help you review and practice these skills.

Every complete sentence is made up of at least one clause. As you have learned, a main clause can stand alone as a sentence.

Examples   I tossed a penny into the fountain.

I made a wish.

A sentence can contain more than one main clause.

Example   <u>I tossed a penny into the fountain</u>, and <u>I made a wish</u>.

A subordinate clause does not express a complete thought, so it cannot stand alone as a sentence.

Examples   when I thought about the wish

which is a secret

Subordinate clauses depend on main clauses to make up a complete sentence. A subordinate clause can come before, after, or in the middle of a main clause.

Examples   <u>When I thought about the wish</u>, <u>I smiled dreamily</u>.
                subordinate clause   *main clause*

<u>A wish is a gift</u> <u>that you give yourself</u>.
  main clause   *sub. clause*

<u>I hope my wish</u>, <u>which is a secret</u>, <u>comes true</u> .
  main clause   *sub. clause*   *main clause cont'd.*

A sentence can contain more than one subordinate clause.

Example   <u>When I left the fountain</u>, <u>I was happy</u>
          sub. clause   *main clause*

<u>because I had made a wish</u>.
    sub. clause

Identify Main and Subordinate Clauses

Label each item *main* for *main clause* or *subordinate* for *subordinate clause*.

Example   <u>subordinate</u> Because customer service is very important to us.

_____ **1.** When you arrive for work.

_____ **2.** The time clock is outside the manager's office.

_____ **3.** Hairnets, name badges, and smocks must be worn at all times.

_____ **4.** Which are part of your work uniform.

_____ **5.** Whenever you greet a customer.

Use Clauses Correctly

Decide whether each item contains an error in the use of clauses. Rewrite the item, correcting the error. If the item is already correct, write *no change*.

Examples   Madge planted a flower garden. When she was only five years old.

Madge planted a flower garden when she was only five years old.

She enjoys the sun, the plants, and even the dirt, which are all part of nature.

no change

1. Since school let out. Madge has been working at JJ's Plant Nursery.

2. She waters all the plants each morning, and she sets out new stock.

3. Her favorites are the herbs. Which can be grown in windowsill gardens.

4. A city dweller can have a fine garden in an arrangement of tiny pots.

5. As she learns their names. She buys one of each herb. That tempts her taste buds.

Uses of Subordinate Clauses

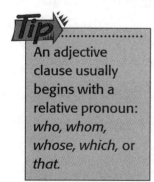

Tip

An adjective clause usually begins with a relative pronoun: *who, whom, whose, which,* or *that.*

In a sentence, a subordinate clause can be used as an adjective, an adverb, or a noun.

An ***adjective clause*** is used to modify a noun or pronoun.

Examples   The cologne <u>that Langston is wearing</u> smells great.

Give me a list of those <u>who bought a yearbook</u>.

When an adjective clause is not essential to the meaning of the sentence, it is set off by a comma or commas.

Examples   This is Carlos, <u>whom you already met</u>.

My cousin, <u>whom you already met</u>, is named Carlos.

When an adjective clause is essential to the meaning, it is not set off by commas.

Example   This is the boy <u>whose arm was broken</u>.

To learn more about using commas with clauses, turn to pages 74–77 in this book.

An ***adverb clause*** modifies a verb, an adjective, or an adverb.

Examples   <u>Before I left</u>, I grabbed an apple. *(adverb phrase modifying a verb)*

This movie is longer <u>than I expected</u>. *(adverb phrase modifying an adjective)*

Carmen danced as gracefully <u>as her instructor dances</u>. *(adverb phrase modifying an adverb)*

A ***noun clause*** is used as a noun in a sentence.

Examples   <u>What Raul saw</u> surprised him. (subject of sentence)

I'll eat <u>whatever you cook</u>. (direct object of the verb <u>eat</u>)

Jill wrote an essay about <u>why pesticides are dangerous</u>. *(object of the preposition <u>about</u>)*

The OGT Writing will not ask you to identify a subordinate clause as an adjective, adverb, or noun. Instead, the OGT will test your ability to recognize errors in the usage of these kinds of clauses and to choose the best correction of an error. Understanding how the clauses are used in sentences will help you identify and correct errors.

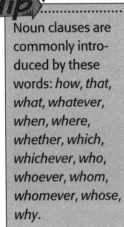

Identify Subordinate Clauses and the Words They Modify

In the following sentences, each subordinate clause is used as an adjective or adverb. Underline each subordinate clause. Then, draw an arrow from the clause to the word it modifies.

Example   An Ohio festival <u>that is especially for twins</u> is the Twins Day Festival.

1. After the glaciers of the Ice Age melted, ancient peoples settled Ohio.

2. Ohio, which is the birthplace of eight U.S. presidents, has 88 counties.

3. Judith Resnik and Nancy Currie are astronauts who were born in Ohio.

4. Ohio's role in the Civil War was larger than you realize.

5. The black racer snake is called the "farmer's friend" because it eats rodents.

Write Noun Clauses

Use the word in parentheses to write a noun clause to complete each sentence.

Example (*where*) Do you know <u>where I left my school ID card</u> ?

6. (*whomever*) Lend the sunscreen lotion to _____ .

7. (*how*) I don't know _____ .

8. (*when*) A pleasant time in my life was _____ .

9. (*What*) _____ is a tall glass of ice water.

10. (*that*) The surgeon remembered _____ .

Multiple Choice

The following passage is made up of main and subordinate clauses. However, most clauses have not been joined together properly to form logical sentences. Look at each underlined part and decide the best change to make to that part. If no change is best, choose NO CHANGE.

Melting Pot or Mixing Pot?

Since the first European settlers began trickling onto America's <u>shores. Various</u> races and peoples have
             1
mixed together in this land. As a result, America has been called a melting pot.

_____ **1. A.** NO CHANGE
       B. shores. Since various
       C. shores, and various
       D. shores, various

"Melting pot" <u>implies. That</u> everyone mingles and
               2

_____ **2. A.** NO CHANGE
       B. implies that
       C. implies, and that
       D. implies, which

melts <u>together. Everyone becomes</u> one people with one _____
3

3. A. NO CHANGE
B. together everyone becomes
C. together, and they become
D. together, and as they become

identity. If you labeled <u>them. You</u> would use one label _____
4

for everyone: American. Sure, you have Irish immi-

grants, Chinese Americans, Hispanics, and African

Americans. Each group brings a mix of cultural

customs, foods, and <u>heritage. What is</u> all stirred into the _____
5

pot that is America.

4. A. NO CHANGE
B. them, you
C. them, and you
D. them, which you

5. A. NO CHANGE
B. heritage, is
C. heritage, and what is
D. heritage, which is

Some <u>believe. People</u> and identities should _____
6

6. A. NO CHANGE
B. believe, and people
C. believe that people
D. believe which people

melt <u>together. Until</u> everyone is just alike. Others _____
7

7. A. NO CHANGE
B. together as
C. together until
D. together, and until

<u>disagree. They</u> say it is not as <u>simple. As</u> some think. _____
89

Each group should keep its cultural identity along with

an identity as an American. In this view, America is

8. A. NO CHANGE
B. disagree, than they
C. disagree they
D. disagree that they

9. A. NO CHANGE
B. simple than
C. simple, and
D. simple as

not so much a melting pot as a mixing <u>pot. What</u> is _____
10

your opinion?

10. A. NO CHANGE
B. pot, what
C. pot, which
D. pot, and

Short Answer

Use the checklist to answer the following question.

Writer's Checklist

✓ Verb Tense
✓ Verb Conjugation
✓ Clauses

Although Marshall has wrote many poems over the years. He has never had one of his poems published.

You have been asked by a fellow student to peer edit the above sentences. Using the checklist, give the writer feedback by identifying the two rules that apply to the errors in the sentences. Then rewrite them correctly.

_____

_____

_____

_____

_____

_____

_____

_____

Look & Learn

In the previous lesson, you learned about using clauses to form complete sentences. Another element of sentences is the phrase. A phrase is a word group used as a single part of speech. Its purpose is to add detail to a sentence. Always part of a clause, a phrase cannot stand alone as a complete sentence.

In the Spotlight

The Phrase

A *phrase* has two main characteristics:

- It is used as a single part of speech
- It does not contain both a subject and its verb.

Examples   on the chalkboard
to learn the definition

A phrase can come at the beginning, middle, or end of a sentence.

Examples   **Snoring gently**, Dad slept.

The cabana **beside the ocean** is Henry's.

My hobby is **collecting baseball cards**.

You studied verb phrases in Lesson 3.1, "Verb Tense." Two additional categories of phrases are *prepositional phrases* and *verbal phrases*. The OGT Writing requires you to use these kinds of phrases correctly. For the test, you will not be asked to label the types of phrases. Rather, you will be asked to recognize errors in the use of phrases and to correct errors. Knowing the kinds of phrases and their uses will help you succeed on the OGT.

Prepositional Phrases

A **prepositional phrase** consists of a preposition, its object, and any modifiers of the object.

Examples   A freight train rumbled **into town**. (*The preposition into takes town as its object.*)

What is **inside the blue box**? (*The preposition inside takes box as its object. The and blue modify box.*)

An object of a preposition may be compound.

Examples   Jasmine wrote thank-you notes **to <u>Ronny</u> and <u>Sam</u>**. *(The preposition <u>to</u> takes <u>Ronny</u> and <u>Sam</u> as its compound object.)*

With the little <u>boy</u> and the big <u>dog</u>, the outing was an adventure. *(The preposition <u>With</u> takes <u>boy</u> and <u>dog</u> as its compound object.)*

Commonly Used Prepositions

about, along, along with, around, behind, beneath, beside, between, by, down, for, from, in, in front of, inside, instead of, near, next to, on, out, outside, over, through, to, under, until, with, without

---

Write Prepositional Phrases

Write a prepositional phrase to complete each sentence. Refer to the list of prepositions above, or think of other prepositions.

Example   A colorful pile of jelly beans spilled *from the jar* .

1. After arriving at the ballpark, I sat _____ .

2. Did you ask the clerk for the price _____ ?

3. The locker _____ is assigned to me.

4. After looking _____ , I ordered soup and salad.

5. Lorrine found her tennis racket _____ .

A prepositional phrase that modifies a noun or a pronoun is called an **adjective phrase**. It tells *which one* or *what kind*.

Examples   Jojo opened a jar **of red paint**. *(<u>Of red paint</u> modifies the noun <u>jar</u>, telling what kind of jar.)*

I can't reach the one **on the top shelf**. *(<u>On the top shelf</u> modifies the pronoun <u>one</u>, telling which one.)*

Two or more adjective phrases may modify the same word.

Example   I can't reach the one **in the back on the top shelf**.

An adjective phrase may modify the object in another prepositional phrase.

Example   I can't reach the one **on the top shelf** **of the cabinet**.
adjective phrase   *adjective phrase*

Identify Adjective Phrases and the Words They Modify

Underline the adjective phrase in each sentence. Then draw an arrow from the phrase to the word it modifies. One sentence has two adjective phrases.

Example   All the CDs <u>on the rack</u> <u>beside the cash register</u> are half price.

1. Would you like a slice of sweet potato pie?

2. An invitation to Hamlin's party was a welcome surprise.

3. The burglar alarm inside the store released an ear-piercing shriek.

4. Here are a few dollars for snacks and drinks.

5. Your homework is the exercise at the end of the chapter.

A prepositional phrase that modifies a verb, an adjective, or an adverb is called an **adverb phrase**.

Examples   A sleek dolphin leaped **out of the water**. *(The adverb phrase modifies the verb <u>leaped</u>.)*

Its body was beautiful **in the sun**. *(The adverb phrase modifies the adjective <u>beautiful</u>.)*

It moved effortlessly **for such a large creature**. *(The adverb phrase modifies the adverb <u>effortlessly</u>.)*

Adverb phrases tell *when, where, why, how,* or *to what extent*.

Examples   Linnea awoke **during the night**. *(Linnea awoke when? <u>During the night</u>.)*

She opened the refrigerator **for a snack**. *(She opened the refrigerator why? <u>For a snack</u>.)*

She dipped **into the ice cream**. *(She dipped where? <u>Into the ice cream</u>.)*

With pleasure, she ate the chocolate treat. *(She ate how? <u>With pleasure</u>.)*

She stayed awake **for an hour**. *(She stayed awake to what extent? <u>For an hour</u>.)*

Identify Adverb Phrases and the Words They Modify

Underline the adverb phrase in each sentence. Then draw an arrow from the phrase to the word it modifies.

Example   An American citizen can vote <u>at age eighteen</u>.

1. Jumping high, Paige threw the basketball through the hoop.

2. My grandfather's life is inspiring to my sister and me.

3. Without hesitation, Jamal offered a helping hand.

4. Mikey kicks a football powerfully for a fifteen-year-old.

5. My parents adopted me soon after my birth.

Verbals and Verbal Phrases

The **verbal** gets its name from the word *verb* because verbals are formed from verbs. However, a verbal is not used as a verb. Instead, a verbal is used as a noun, an adjective, or an adverb.

Example 1   **Swimming** is good exercise. *(verbal used as a noun)*

   Swimming is a noun formed from the verb *swim*. *Swimming* is the subject of the sentence.

Example 2   Do you like **fried** potatoes? *(verbal used as an adjective)*

   Fried is an adjective formed from the verb *fry*. *Fried* modifies *potatoes*.

Example 3   Elena is always quick **to laugh**. *(verbal used as an adverb)*

   To laugh is an adverb formed from the verb *laugh*. *To laugh* modifies *quick*.

The three kinds of verbals are gerunds, participles, and infinitives.

- **Gerunds** are used as nouns. Example 1 above shows a gerund.
- **Participles** are used as adjectives. Example 2 above shows a participle.
- **Infinitives** are used as nouns, adjectives, or adverbs. Example 3 above shows an infinitive.

A **verbal phrase** is made up of a verbal and its modifiers and complements.

Examples   **Swimming ten laps** is good exercise. *(verbal phrase used as a noun)*

   Do you like potatoes **fried in peanut oil**? *(verbal phrase used as an adjective)*

Elena is always quick **to laugh joyfully**. *(verbal phrase used as an adverb)*

Keep reading to find out more about each kind of verbal and verbal phrase.

Tip

Gerunds always end in *-ing*.

A **gerund** is a verb form used as a noun in a sentence.

Examples   Joshua enjoys **writing**. *(Writing is a verbal formed from the verb write. Writing is used as a noun—specifically, as the direct object of the verb enjoys.)*

Cheating is not an option. *(Cheating is a verbal formed from the verb cheat. Cheating is used as a noun—the subject of the sentence.)*

I live for **dancing**. *(Dancing is a verbal formed from the verb dance. Dancing is used as a noun—the object of the preposition for.)*

Try It Out

Identify Gerunds

Underline the gerund in each sentence.

Example   At times, <u>crying</u> is a good release for pent-up emotions.

1. One of Oscar's favorite sports is boxing.
2. For fishing, Uncle Chester recommends worms as bait.
3. Sanding will smooth the surface of this rough wood.
4. Brittany gave studying her full concentration.
5. "That whispering must stop!" said Professor Porter.

A **gerund phrase** is made up of a gerund and its modifiers and complements.

Examples   Joshua enjoys **writing limericks**. *(The gerund is writing. The gerund phrase is used as the direct object of the verb enjoys.)*

The wilting of the flowers signaled a dry spell. *(The gerund is wilting. The gerund phrase is used as the subject of the sentence.)*

Instead of **buying a lunch**, I bring a sandwich from home. *(The gerund is buying. The gerund phrase is used as the object of the preposition Instead of.)*

Try It Out

Identify Gerund Phrases

Underline the gerund phrase in each sentence.

Example   Was <u>learning a foreign language</u> difficult for you?

6. Sandy's daily chore is carrying out the garbage.
7. As I learned recently, gossiping about a friend can backfire on you.

8. "Thank you for babysitting the children," Mr. Jackson said.

9. Many people fear speaking in front of large audiences.

10. Eating a vegetarian diet is becoming more common nowadays.

A **participle** is a verb form that can be used as an adjective. A **participial phrase** is made up of a participle and its modifiers and complements. Participial phrases are used as adjectives in sentences.

Tip

Most participles end in *-ing, -d,* or *-ed.* For more information on participles, turn to Lesson 3.1 in this book.

Examples   **Painted**, the bicycle looks much better. (*The participle Painted modifies bicycle.*)

Painted shiny red, the bicycle looks much better. (*The participial phrase Painted shiny red modifies bicycle.*)

I watched the puppy **running**. (*The participle running modifies puppy.*)

I watched the puppy **running after the boy**. (*The participial phrase running after the boy modifies puppy.*)

Identify Participles and the Words They Modify

Underline the participle in each sentence. Draw an arrow from the participle to the word it modifies.

Example   Are <u>flying</u> saucers fact or fiction?

1. Amazed, Francis stared at the small, brown alien.

2. The smiling creature waved a long brown hand at her.

3. The other teenagers, frozen, watched silently.

4. Flashing lights on the spacecraft lit the area.

5. In its other hand, the alien carried a small carved box.

Identify Participial Phrases and the Words They Modify

Underline the participial phrase in each sentence. Draw an arrow from the participial phrase to the word it modifies.

Example   The morning sun, <u>glistening on the lake</u>, was awesome.

6. Flapping its wings, the hawk rose into the air.

7. A mockingbird, perched on a branch, sang cheerfully.

8. Swayed by a light breeze, treetops danced.

9. A frog leaping off a lily pad made a sudden splash.

10. Holding my camera steady, I snapped photographs.

Tip

An infinitive is **to** plus a **verb**. Remember that *to* plus a noun or a pronoun is a prepositional phrase, not an infinitive.

An **infinitive** is a verb form that can be used as a noun, an adjective, or an adverb. Most infinitives begin with *to,* as in *to learn.*

Examples   **To learn** is admirable. *(infinitive used as a noun)*
The infinitive *To learn* is the subject of the sentence.

My goal **to excel** is realistic. *(infinitive used as an adjective)*
The infinitive *to excel* modifies the noun *goal.*

I am willing **to study**. *(infinitive used as an adverb)*
The infinitive *to study* modifies the adjective *willing.*

Form Infinitives

Use the verb in parentheses to form an infinitive. Then write the infinitive on the line provided to complete the sentence.

Example   The homework ___*to complete*___ is written on the chalkboard. *(complete)*

1. Quiet! I am trying _____ now. *(study)*

2. _____ is one of the most important qualities in a friend. *(forgive)*

3. The one _____ about the musical tryouts is Ms. Terrence. *(ask)*

4. Why are you afraid _____ ? *(fly)*

5. Unwisely, I tried _____ to Principal Vegas. *(lie)*

An **infinitive phrase** is made up of an infinitive and its modifiers and complements. The phrase is used as a noun, an adjective, or an adverb in a sentence.

Examples   **To learn grammar** is admirable. *(infinitive phrase used as a noun)*
The infinitive phrase is the subject of the sentence.

My goal **to excel on the OGT** is realistic. *(infinitive phrase used as an adjective)*
The infinitive phrase modifies the noun *goal.*

I am willing **to study regularly**. *(infinitive phrase used as an adverb)*
The infinitive phrase modifies the adjective *willing.*

Identify Infinitive Phrases

Underline the infinitives and infinitive phrases in the passage (there is a total of ten). Not every sentence contains an infinitive or infinitive phrase.

Example   Have you ever stopped <u>to think about the homeless</u>?

Each day in our communities, homeless individuals try to find food and shelter. Whether you see them or not, they are out there, attempting to scratch out an existence. But solving the problems of the homeless is a job best left to adults, right? Think again. It shouldn't be that easy for a teen to dismiss the situation.

While it is true that adults fill influential roles such as mayor, police chief, and social worker, there are other roles to pursue. They include volunteer, activist, and problem solver. Around the country, many teens seek out ways to assist those in need. They search the Internet to find local shelters and relief organizations. They ask teachers and librarians to direct them to volunteer opportunities. They work in soup kitchens, they volunteer to staff donation drives, and they ask friends to donate clothing and food to worthy causes. Those who try to make a difference *do* make a difference.

As a writer, you can strengthen your sentences and paragraphs by using prepositional and verbal phrases. When used correctly, phrases help sentences convey ideas clearly and concisely. For instance, choppy sentences can be combined by putting some information into a phrase. Information in repetitive sentences can be streamlined by using phrases to form one concise sentence.

Choppy	He had researched tropical rain forests. It was for his essay. It added vital details.
Revised	His research **on tropical rain forests** added vital details **to his essay**. (*Prepositional phrases help streamline the information into one concise sentence.*)
Choppy	He pressed a button. He booted up the computer.
Revised	**Pressing a button,** he booted up the computer. (*A participial phrase improves the flow of information.*)
Repetitive	He proofread the paragraphs. The paragraphs scrolled across the screen.
Revised	He proofread the paragraphs **scrolling across the screen.** (*A participial phrase eliminates unnecessary repetition.*)

Use Phrases to Revise Sentences

Choose the best revision for each item. If the item is correct as it is, choose NO CHANGE.

Example The party was held on the Fourth of July. It was a family gathering. It was held in the park.

    A. NO CHANGE

    B. The party was held on the Fourth of July. It was a family gathering held in the park.

    (C.) Held on the Fourth of July, the party was a family gathering in the park.

    D. On the Fourth of July, the party was a family gathering. It was held in the park.

1. Geoffrey brought balloons. The balloons were from a party supply store.

    A. NO CHANGE

    B. Geoffrey brought balloons, and they were from a party supply store.

    C. Geoffrey brought balloons. They were brought from a party supply store.

    D. Geoffrey brought balloons from a party supply store.

2. I contributed a kind of firecracker. We call this firecracker a "sparkler."

    A. NO CHANGE

    B. I contributed a kind of firecracker. This firecracker is called a "sparkler."

    C. I contributed a kind of firecracker called a "sparkler."

    D. I contributed a kind of firecracker. It is called a "sparkler."

3. Mom baked a white cake. Then Mom decorated it with red and blue berries.

    A. NO CHANGE

    B. Baking a white cake. Mom decorated it with red and blue berries.

    C. Mom baked a white cake. Decorated with red and blue berries.

    D. After baking a white cake, Mom decorated it with red and blue berries.

4. We had a plan. We wanted to celebrate. It was a classic American holiday.

    A. NO CHANGE

B. Our plan was to celebrate a classic American holiday.

C. Our plan to celebrate. It was a classic American holiday.

D. We had a plan. To celebrate a classic American holiday.

5. The day, filled with fun and games, was a success.

A. NO CHANGE

B. The day was filled with fun and games. It was a success.

C. The day was filled with fun and games, and it was a success.

D. Filled with fun and games. The day was a success.

Multiple Choice

In the following passage, most of the underlined parts can be improved by using a prepositional or verbal phrase. Select the best revision for each underlined part. If an item is correct as is, select NO CHANGE.

Imagine <u>a train wreck. You hear the wreck happen</u>
                                    1
near your house. You realize you are the only one

_____ 1. **A.** NO CHANGE
B. hearing a train wreck happen
C. a train wreck. The wreck happens
D. a train wreck. It happens

<u>available. Going for help.</u> This very emergency
              2

_____ 2. **A.** NO CHANGE
B. going for help available.
C. available to go for help.
D. available for help.

happened <u>to fifteen-year-old Kate Shelley.</u>
                              3

_____ 3. **A.** NO CHANGE
B. to Shelley.
C. to Kate.
D. fifteen-year-old Kate Shelley.

<u>She stayed up late one night. She</u> listened to a rain
                    4
storm rage outside. At nearly midnight, she heard

_____ 4. **A.** NO CHANGE
B. Staying up late one night. She
C. To stay up late one night. She
D. Staying up late one night, she

Using Grammar **123**

Engine Number <u>Eleven. The engine climbed</u> the slope to _____
5

Honey Creek Bridge near her house. Then a terrible

crash sounded, and water hissed as the hot engine

<u>fell. It fell from the broken bridge</u> into cold waters. Kate _____
6

knew that the midnight express, a passenger train,

<u>was due. It would cross</u> the bridge soon. <u>Crawling across</u> _____
78

the <u>700-foot-long Des Moines River Bridge,</u> Kate reached _____
8

the Moingona Station. <u>She announced the crash. It was</u> _____
9

<u>Number Eleven. After that</u> she learned the midnight
9

express had already been halted. Immediately she led a

5. A. NO CHANGE
B. Eleven. It climbed
C. Eleven climbing. It climbed
D. Eleven climbing

6. A. NO CHANGE
B. fell from the broken bridge
C. fell. The engine fell from the broken bridge
D. fell. Falling from the broken bridge

7. A. NO CHANGE
B. was due. It would be crossing
C. was due to cross
D. was due. Crossing

8. A. NO CHANGE
B. Crawled across the 700-foot-long Des Moines River Bridge,
C. To crawl across the 700-foot-long Des Moines River Bridge,
D. Crawl across the 700-foot-long Des Moines River Bridge,

9. A. NO CHANGE
B. Announcing the crash of Number Eleven. After that
C. She announced the crash, Number Eleven. After that
D. After announcing the crash of Number Eleven,

rescue party, saving two Engine Eleven <u>crew members.</u> ——
                                        10

<u>That was a fateful night. It was July 6, 1881.</u>
                    10

10. A. NO CHANGE
  B. crew members on that fateful night of July 6, 1881.
  C. crew members. That was a fateful night, July 6, 1881.
  D. crew members, being a fateful night of July 6, 1881.

Short Answer
Use the checklist to answer the following question.

Writer's Checklist

✓ Verb Tense
✓ Phrases
✓ Clauses

After the movie ends, we went to a diner and ordered a hot fudge sundae, and it had whipped cream and cherries on top.

You have been asked by a fellow student to peer edit the above sentence. Using the checklist, give the writer feedback by identifying the two rules to apply in order to improve the sentence. Then rewrite the sentence correctly.

_____

_____

_____

_____

_____

_____

_____

_____

Lesson 3.4   Modifiers

 **& Learn**

Modifiers help us get our exact meaning across in speaking and writing. Look for the modifiers in these two conversations:

> *Jamez:* Have you seen my shirt?
> *Dad:* Which shirt?
> *Jamez:* My **new black** shirt!

> *Elizabeth:* Did you finish the homework?
> *Trenton:* What homework?
> *Elizabeth:* The homework **that Mr. Edwards gave us**.

In both cases, a speaker uses at least one modifier to make the meaning of another word more specific.

In the Spotlight

Modifiers

A *modifier* is a word or word group that makes the meaning of another word or word group more precise. A modifier can consist of one word, a phrase, or a clause.

Examples   I stepped on a **sharp** tack. *(one-word modifier)*

A tack **from my bulletin board** had fallen. *(modifying phrase)*

The tack **that fell** hurt my foot. *(modifying clause)*

The two kinds of modifiers are adjectives and adverbs. **Adjective modifiers** make the meanings of nouns and pronouns more specific.

Examples   My **slick** shoes skidded.

Visibility **in the downpour** declined.

Adverb modifiers make the meanings of verbs, adjectives, and adverbs more specific.

Examples   My shoes skidded **suddenly**.

Visibility declined **as rain poured**.

The OGT Writing requires you to use modifiers correctly. You should be able to

- identify modifiers in sentences
- find the word or word group modified
- recognize a modifier used incorrectly
- choose the best revision for an incorrectly used modifier

One-Word Modifiers

A modifier may consist of only one word. A one-word **adjective modifier** usually is placed right before the noun or pronoun it modifies.

Examples   The **tan** one matches the skirt.

Only Shelley Smith can speak German.

An adjective must be placed as closely as possible to the word it modifies. Notice the different meanings created when the modifier *only* is placed at different points in the sentence.

Only Shelley Smith can speak German. (*Shelley Smith is the only one who can speak German.*)

Shelley Smith can speak **only** German. (*German is the only language Shelley Smith can speak.*)

Shelley Smith can **only** speak German. (*Shelley Smith can speak German, but she can't read or write it.*)

Identify Adjectives and the Words They Modify
Underline the adjective in each sentence. Then draw an arrow from the adjective to the word or word group it modifies. One sentence has two adjectives.

Example   Irritated, I yelled at my friend.

1. During the recital, Maxine played a complex tune on the piano.

2. Hurrying, Jordan Connelly barely caught the bus this morning.

3. At the sound of the alarm, calm students filed from the building.

4. Since my best friend moved away, I have tried to make new friends.

5. The winners, triumphant, received trophies and ribbons.

An **adverb modifier** may come before or after the verb, adjective, or adverb it modifies.

Examples   The debate team practiced **faithfully**. *(modifying a verb)*

Your fingernails are **extremely** long. *(modifying an adjective)*

Music blared **incredibly** loudly. *(modifying an adverb)*

In some sentences, the meaning is clear whether the adverb is next to the word it modifies or farther away.

Examples   **Kindly,** Grandpa patted my shoulder.

Grandpa **kindly** patted my shoulder.

Grandpa patted my shoulder **kindly**.

In other sentences, the meaning changes depending on where the adverb is placed. In these cases, the adverb must be placed as close as possible to the word it modifies.

Examples   **Surprisingly**, Felix handled the crisis calmly. *(It is a surprise that Felix handled the crisis calmly.)*

Felix handled the crisis **surprisingly** calmly. *(The degree of calmness is surprising.)*

Identify Adverbs and the Words They Modify

Underline the adverb in each sentence. Then draw an arrow from the adverb to the word or word group it modifies. One sentence has two adverbs.

Example   In centuries past, jesters <u>often</u> entertained the royal court.

Frequently a jester's outfit consisted of a many-pointed cap, multicolored clothing, and bells. Jesters, sometimes called fools, were a part of the courts of Egyptian pharaohs. Among the ancient Aztecs of Mexico, jesters regularly provided comic relief to their patrons (sponsors). England's royal courts historically enjoyed jesters' jokes, performances, and madness—real or pretended. Some jesters were truly mad rather than merely pretending madness.

Some modifiers can function as either an adjective or an adverb. It depends on how you use the modifier in a sentence.

Adjective   I want the **last** muffin!

Adverb   Miranda arrived **last**.

Adjective   **Only** the girls went on the campout. (*No more than the girls went on the campout.*)

Adverb   The girls **only** went on the campout. (*They did no more than go on the campout.*)

Identify One-Word Modifiers and the Words They Modify

Underline the adjectives and adverbs in the sentences below. Then draw an arrow from each modifier to the word or word group it modifies.

Example   In the Alps each year, approximately 150 people die in avalanches.

1. During World War II, loud gunfire in the Tyrolean Alps caused deadly avalanches.

2. Glistening ice and beautiful snow routinely cause unexpected dangers.

3. Did you know that, in extremely cold temperatures, eyeballs can freeze?

4. With their acutely sensitive noses, dogs can sniff out lost people in snowy areas.

5. Seemingly solid sheets of ice on lakes and ponds can crack suddenly under weight.

Modifying Phrases

Like one-word modifiers, modifying phrases are used as either adjectives or adverbs.

Adjectives   **Applauding wildly**, the audience stood. (*This participial phrase modifies the noun <u>audience</u>.*)

The time **for a decision** is now. (*This prepositional phrase modifies the noun <u>time</u>.*)

Someone **to help you** will be nearby. *(This infinitive phrase modifies the pronoun Someone.)*

Adverbs   The audience stood **to its feet**. *(This prepositional phrase modifies the verb stood.)*

Cinderella's foot was small enough **to fit the slipper**. *(This infinitive phrase modifies the adverb enough.)*

Which antique is costlier **than the other**? *(This prepositional phrase modifies the adjective costlier.)*

> **Tip**
> A phrase is a word group that does not contain both a subject and its verb. A phrase is used as a single part of speech in a sentence. To learn more about phrases, turn to Lesson 3.3 in this book.

Identify Phrases and the Words They Modify

Underline the phrases in the sentences below. Then draw an arrow from each phrase to the word or word group it modifies. A hint at the end of each sentence tells you how many phrases to locate in that sentence.

Example   Should an individual be required <u>to take responsibility</u> for <u>preventing the spread of illness</u>? *(2 phrases)*

1. Typhoid is caused by a tiny bacterium impossible to see without a microscope. *(3 phrases)*

2. A typhoid fever epidemic erupted in 1904 in Oyster Bay, New York. *(2 phrases)*

3. Working energetically, health officials traced the epidemic to its source. *(2 phrases)*

4. Mary Mallon, employed as a household cook, was a carrier of the typhoid bacillus. *(2 phrases)*

5. Locating the household, authorities realized that Mary had fled. *(1 phrase)*

6. As Mary moved around, authorities continued to track her. *(1 phrase)*

7. For a time, Mary was committed to a quarantine center by health officials. *(3 phrases)*

8. Later Mary, released from the center, continued to spread typhoid by working as a cook. *(4 phrases)*

9. Typhoid epidemics at a sanitarium and a maternity hospital were traced to Mary. *(2 phrases)*

10. Finally health officials returned "Typhoid Mary" to the quarantine facility, and she died there in 1938. *(2 phrases)*

Modifying Clauses

Like modifying words and phrases, a modifying clause may be used as an adjective or an adverb.

Adjectives   Nobody **who arrived late** was allowed inside. *(This clause modifies the pronoun Nobody.)*

              The quiz, **which was a surprise**, was easy. *(This clause modifies the noun quiz.)*

Adverbs   **Before night fell**, I locked the windows. *(This clause modifies the verb locked.)*

              The engine ran poorly **until Hank tuned it**. *(This clause modifies the adverb poorly.)*

- A clause is a word group that contains both a subject and its verb.
- Clauses used as adjectives begin with the pronouns *who, whom, whose, which,* and *that.*
- Clauses used as adverbs begin with words such as *after, although, before, if, since, unless, until, when, while,* and others.
- A modifying clause is always a subordinate clause.

To learn more about clauses, turn to Lesson 3.2 in this book.

Identify Modifying Clauses and the Words They Modify

Underline the modifying clauses in the following sentences. Then draw an arrow from each clause to the word or word group it modifies. A hint at the end of each sentence tells you how many clauses to locate in that sentence. (Remember, a modifying clause is a subordinate clause, not a main clause.)

Example   When I enroll in college, I will take courses that the physical education department offers. *(2 clauses)*

1. After school lets out, I am going straight to the soccer field. *(1 clause)*

2. Croquet, which originated in France, is a game that is played with mallets and balls. *(2 clauses)*

3. Your opinion that Ping-Pong is silly offends me. *(1 clause)*

4. Devon, whose father coaches basketball, gave Jay a few tips while they practiced. *(2 clauses)*

5. Once I arrive at school, I have already jogged two miles and showered. *(1 clause)*

6. Try another sport if you don't like track. *(1 clause)*

7. As the team's star pitcher, Yolanda practices until every pitch crosses the plate. *(1 clause)*

8. Take your tennis racket to Reggie, who will tighten the strings that are loose. *(2 clauses)*

9. Since I watched the Olympics on television, I have wanted to learn gymnastics. *(1 clause)*

10. My aunt, whom I adore, is a varsity girls' volleyball coach whose team often wins. *(2 clauses)*

Misplaced Modifiers

Misunderstanding can occur when a modifier is not placed next to the word or word group it modifies.

Misplaced   Choppy and white-capped, the tiny boat fought the waves. *(Is the boat choppy and white-capped?)*

Clear   The tiny boat fought the choppy and white-capped waves. *(The waves are choppy and white-capped.)*

Misplaced **Still warm from the oven**, Erica savored the cookie. *(Is Erica still warm from the oven?)*

Clear Erica savored the cookie, **still warm from the oven**. *(The cookie is still warm from the oven.)*

Misplaced Gabrielle dabbed the perfume on each wrist **that Lorne bought her**. *(Did Lorne buy wrists for her?)*

Clear Gabrielle dabbed the perfume **that Lorne bought her** on each wrist. *(Lorne bought her the perfume.)*

To decide whether a sentence has a misplaced modifier, follow these steps.

1. Underline each modifier.
2. Draw an arrow to the nearest word it could modify.
3. Ask, "Does this modifier logically modify that word?"
4. If the answer is no, you probably have pinpointed a misplaced modifier.
5. If the answer is yes, the modifier is most likely used correctly.

Identify Misplaced Modifiers

Underline each modifying phrase and clause. Then draw an arrow from the modifier to the word or word group it modifies. If a modifier is misplaced, write *misplaced* above it.

Examples Green bamboo grew <u>in the red pot</u> <u>with narrow leaves</u>. *misplaced*

Marcy goes <u>to the library</u>, <u>where she browses the Internet</u>.

1. Topped with marshmallows, we drank steaming hot chocolate.

2. When it burned, our kitchen filled with the smell of the fish.

3. I gave the birdbath, coated with algae, a good scrub with a brush.

4. Foaming at the mouth, Ricardo suspected that the dog was dangerous.

5. The band has a sharp new uniform, which is open to new members.

6. The song that you wrote for my birthday touched my heart.

7. A sculpture was the centerpiece of the party made of ice.

8. To study Caitlin borrowed notes for the test from a classmate.

9. Quinn changes the oil in the car that his father drives.

10. Stefanie found a bracelet on the sidewalk that someone had lost.

To revise a sentence containing a misplaced modifier, place the modifier as close as possible to the word it modifies.

Misplaced   Please hang these posters on the walls, **which announce the carnival**.

Clear   Please hang these posters, **which announce the carnival**, on the walls.

Misplaced   The airplane glinted in the sun **roaring overhead**.

Clear   The airplane, **roaring overhead**, glinted in the sun.

Clear   **Roaring overhead**, the airplane glinted in the sun.

Sometimes, the best revision of a misplaced modifier is not obvious. Try a couple of different versions of the sentence until you have a revision with no misplaced modifiers.

Misplaced   Barbara found a surprising note in her locker **from a secret admirer**.

Misplaced   Barbara found a surprising note from a secret admirer **in her locker**.

Clear   **In her locker**, Barbara found a surprising note **from a secret admirer**.

Revise Sentences to Correct Misplaced Modifiers

Revise each sentence to correct the misplaced modifying phrase or clause.

Example   The guitar had been scratched by someone else that Wendy owned.

The guitar that Wendy owned had been scratched by someone else.

1. The football was a brown blur to Logan, hurtling through the air.

2. I borrowed a pencil from a friend that was sharpened to a point.

3. The art student imagined the finished vase kneading wet clay.

4. Written for teenagers, Donnel found the book fascinating.

---

5. The iced cardboard cake amused the teacher which was a practical joke.

---

6. The dessert tempted Justine, made of shimmering green gelatin.

---

7. The free-throw line is fading that was painted on the basketball court.

---

8. Cheerleaders formed a pyramid at the pep rally of human bodies.

---

9. Anyone can pick it up who bought a ticket in Ms. Sherman's office.

---

10. An exchange student is now attending my small-town Ohio high school from Italy.

Dangling Modifiers

A **dangling modifier** is a modifier that does not clearly and logically modify a word or word group in the sentence.

Dangling	**Broken**, a repair was needed. (*Is the repair broken?*)
Clear	**Broken**, the **microscope** needed a repair.
Dangling	**Waking up early**, the day was cool and fresh. (*The day cannot wake up early.*)
Clear	**Waking up early**, the **campers** noticed the day was cool and fresh.
Dangling	**Shocked by the scandal**, an investigation was begun. (*Is the investigation shocked?*)
Clear	**Shocked by the scandal**, the **chief** began an investigation.

To decide whether a sentence contains a dangling modifier, follow these steps.

1. Use common sense. Ask yourself, "Does this sentence sound strange to me?" Often (but not always) you'll recognize a dangling modifier because the sentence's meaning seems incomplete, odd, or even ridiculous.
2. Underline each modifier in the sentence.
3. Locate the word whose meaning the modifier makes more specific.
4. If you find the modified word, double-check that the modifier *logically* modifies it.
5. If you cannot locate a word logically modified, the modifier is probably dangling.

Identify Dangling Modifiers

Underline the modifier that begins each sentence. If the modifier logically modifies a word or word group in the sentence, draw an arrow to it. If the modifier is dangling, write *dangling* above it.

Examples   <u>Inspired by good role models</u>, anything is possible.
dangling

<u>Making a slimy trail</u>, the slug inched across a rock.

1. Soaked, fresh towels were the top priority.

2. After studying all week, the test was easy.

3. Beloved by many, Shel Silverstein is the author of *Where the Side-walk Ends.*

4. Fussy and cranky, a short nap helped.

5. Entertained by great singing, the evening was a success.

6. Squeaking quietly, the mouse's exercise wheel spun rapidly.

7. Grabbing a tissue, the sneeze was due to hay fever.

8. Before jumping in, the swimmer tested the water's temperature.

9. Rapidly typing, the paper filled with well-formed paragraphs.

10. Hearing about the OGT Writing, the class began preparing for it.

To correct a dangling modifier, add, remove, or replace words in the sentence so the modifier logically modifies a word or word group.

Dangling	**Exhausted**, a few minutes of rest were in order.
Clear	Exhausted, the **builders** thought a few minutes of rest were in order.

Dangling	**Walking through school hallways**, greetings were called out.
Clear	Walking through school hallways, **friends** called out greetings.

When a modifier begins a sentence, make sure the word or word group it modifies comes directly after it. Add or rearrange words until the modifier is used logically.

Dangling	**Although new to the area**, the streets were easy to navigate. (*The modifier does not logically modify a word in the sentence.*)
Dangling	**Although new to the area**, the streets were easy **for us** to navigate. (*Even though <u>for us</u> was added, the modifier still does not clearly modify a word in the sentence.*)
Clear	**Although new to the area**, **we** discovered the streets were easy to navigate. (<u>We</u> *comes directly after the modifying phrase and is clearly modified by it.*)

Revise Sentences to Correct Dangling Modifiers

Revise each sentence to correct the dangling modifier. In your revised sentence, draw an arrow from the modifier to the word it logically modifies.

Example   Named after his father, the resemblance was striking.

Named after his father, Gilbert had a striking resemblance to him.

1. Held by glue, nothing would fall off the collage.

_____

2. Surfing through television channels, the evening was boring.

_____

3. Injured in the game, paramedics were available immediately.

_____

4. Being honest, a lie is not fair to you.

_____

5. After working together as lab partners, a new friendship developed.

_____

6. Windswept and dusty, plants and irrigation would be an improvement.

_____

7. Surprised by the alarm, only one item was stolen.

_____

8. Marked on Mom's calendar, she never forgets.

_____

9. Overdue at the library, fines were charged.

_____

10. Bashful, a friendly face at the party would have been welcome.

_____

On Your Own Choose the best revision for each underlined part. If the sentence is correct, choose NO CHANGE.

Soaring high in the clouds, the view was

1

spectacular. Eagerly I pressed my nose beside

2

my seat against the window. Puffy and white as cotton,

2

_____ **1. A.** NO CHANGE
B. Soaring high in the clouds, I thought the view
C. Soaring high, the view in the clouds
D. Soaring, the view high in the sky

_____ **2. A.** NO CHANGE
B. against the window, my nose beside my seat
C. beside my seat my nose against the window
D. my nose against the window beside my seat

I observed clouds not far below. Charmed by the
                3

peaceful scene, art supplies came to mind. Pulling
                    4

out my satchel, I rummaged for a pad and pencil.
                   5

Contented, the sketch took shape quickly. It
                6

would look great in the frame on the wall that
                        7
Grandma bought me. Upon my arrival home,
7

Dad could help me with the project. After framing the
8

____ 3. A. NO CHANGE
       B. I observed them not
          far below
       C. not far below I ob-
          served clouds
       D. clouds could be ob-
          served not far below

____ 4. A. NO CHANGE
       B. to my mind came art
          supplies
       C. I thought of my art
          supplies
       D. came to mind my art
          supplies

____ 5. A. NO CHANGE
       B. a pad and pencil
          were rummaged for
       C. rummaging for a pad
          and pencil
       D. for a pad and pencil

____ 6. A. NO CHANGE
       B. Contented, I sketched
       C. Contented, my
          sketch took shape
       D. The sketch, con-
          tented, took shape

____ 7. A. NO CHANGE
       B. on the wall that
          Grandma bought me,
          in the frame
       C. on the wall in the
          frame that Grandma
          bought me
       D. in the frame that
          Grandma bought me
          on the wall

____ 8. A. NO CHANGE
       B. Dad, helping me with
          the project
       C. the project with
          Dad's help
       D. the project could re-
          ceive Dad's help

sketch, <u>it would go in the dining room</u>. The rest of the
9

      9. A. NO CHANGE
           B. the sketch would go in the dining room
           C. in the dining room it would go
           D. we would hang it in the dining room

<u>flight flew by in the blink of an eye three hours long</u>.
10

      10. A. NO CHANGE
           B. flight in the blink of an eye flew by three hours long
           C. flight, three hours long, flew by in the blink of an eye
           D. flight flew by three hours long, in the blink of an eye

Lesson 3.5   Parallel Structure

Look & Learn

Grab a couple of pencils. Got them? Now place them side by side on your desk. Line them up so they are an equal distance apart, from erasers to tips. All done? Excellent! You have just arranged the pencils in a *parallel* structure. You could add five more pencils, and as long as they are lined up equally with the first two, all of them would be arranged in a parallel structure.

So what's the point of this exercise? Just like pencils on your desk, words on your paper can have parallel structure. The key is creating an arrangement of *equal grammatical parts*.

In the Spotlight

Parallel Structure

Parallel structure is the use of the same grammatical form to list items in a series or to present ideas side by side for emphasis.

Items in a series

Not parallel	Nurse Pope's uniform is clean, a light shade of blue, and she just bought it. *(an adjective, a phrase, and a clause)*
Parallel	Nurse Pope's uniform is **clean**, **blue**, and **new**. *(three adjectives)*
Not parallel	We hid Easter eggs in the grass, bushes, and putting them behind rocks. *(a prepositional phrase, a noun, and a participial phrase)*
Parallel	We hid Easter eggs **in the grass**, **under bushes**, and **behind rocks**. *(three prepositional phrases)*

Ideas side by side for emphasis

Not parallel	To grow a garden is communing with nature. *(infinitive phrase and participial phrase)*
Parallel	**To grow a garden** is **to commune with nature**. *(two infinitive phrases)*
Not parallel	Seeing is to believe. *(gerund and infinitive)*
Parallel	**Seeing** is **believing**. *(two gerunds)*

In the examples above, notice how ideas set in parallel structure flow smoothly from one to the next. Each sentence is clear, logical, and pleasing to the ear. In contrast, ideas presented together but not in parallel structure create a choppy effect. The sentences sound awkward because the grammatical parts in the list are not equal or balanced.

The purpose of parallel structure is to balance ideas. You should balance a noun with a noun, an infinitive phrase with an infinitive phrase, a subordinate clause with a subordinate clause, and so on. When you do so, your ideas are balanced, your ideas are parallel in structure, and your writing is clear and correct.

Parallel Words

Nouns, verbs, adjectives, and adverbs are commonly used to form lists or pairs of parallel words.

Examples   **Planes**, **trains**, and **automobiles** fascinate Pete. *(nouns)*

As a child I often **skipped**, **hopped**, and **jumped**. *(verbs)*

My Spanish class is **large** but **friendly**. *(adjectives)*

Slowly, **carefully**, and **creatively**, Hanna designed a dress. *(adverbs)*

To locate nonparallel structure in lists of words or in words set side by side for emphasis, follow these steps:

1. Identify the words in the list or the words set up for emphasis.
2. Identify the part of speech of each word.
3. If the parts of speech are different, you have pinpointed nonparallel structure. If the parts of speech are *all* the same, you have identified parallel structure.

To correct nonparallel structure, choose one part of speech with which to express all words in the list.

Not parallel   Posters, drawings I made, photographs, and colorful banners decorate the walls of my room.

The problem: The list consists of three different forms of items: a noun, a noun modified by a clause, another noun, and a noun modified by an adjective.

The solution: Choose one form to use for all four items in the list. Four nouns would work well.

Parallel   **Posters**, **drawings**, **photographs**, and **banners** decorate the walls of my room.

Not parallel   The strange soup had lumps, goopy, and a greenish color.

The problem: The list consists of three different forms of items: a noun, an adjective, and a noun modified by an adjective.

The solution: Choose one form to use for all items in the list. Adjectives would work well.

Parallel   The strange soup was **lumpy**, **goopy**, and **greenish**.

Not parallel The child's face was sweet, but there was sadness.

The problem: Two ideas are set side by side for emphasis, but the ideas are expressed in different forms—an adjective and a clause.

The solution: Choose one form for both ideas. Two adjectives would work well.

Parallel   The child's face was **sweet** but **sad**.

Identify Parallel and Nonparallel Structure in Words

In each sentence, underline the items in a series or the items set side by side for emphasis. Above the underlined words, write *parallel* or *nonparallel*.

Example   *nonparallel*
        <u>Bouncing</u>, <u>squeaking</u>, and <u>in lurches</u>, the car rounded the curve.

1. The Amazon rain forest is home to jaguars, different types of monkeys, and manatees.

2. During October, Janelle researched, wrote, did a revision, and carefully polished her story.

3. My grades improved slowly and with sureness.

4. Chocolate is happiness.

5. Rapidly, with skill, and hungrily, the otter broke open the clam.

Revise Sentences to Correct Nonparallel Structure in Words

Rewrite all or part of each sentence to correct nonparallel structure.

Example   During World War II, Ohio factories produced aircraft, ships, various kinds of ammunition, and tires made of rubber.

aircraft, ships, ammunition, and tires.

6. We went to see a movie advertised as "slick, a source of fun, and refreshing."

7. Unfortunately my old, slow, not very reliable computer crashed last night.

___

8. Because he was innocent, the suspect answered the officers' questions with truth, honestly, and willingly.

___

9. Dear Fluffy is gone but not to be forgotten.

___

10. Polluted lakes and rivers prevent people from fishing, to swim, and boats.

___

Try It Out

Write Sentences with Parallel Structure

Answer each question by writing a sentence using parallel structure in a series. The word in parentheses specifies the part of speech to use.

Example   How did you learn to play football so well? *(adverbs)*

I practiced regularly, energetically, and fearlessly.

___

11. What foods are on the menu in the cafeteria today? *(nouns)*

___

12. What kind of outfit are you wearing to the dance? *(adjectives)*

___

13. What did he do to the car? *(verbs)*

___

14. How did you cheer for our team? *(adverbs)*

___

15. What things are found in a typical classroom? *(nouns)*

___

Parallel Phrases

Prepositional phrases and verbal phrases are commonly used to form parallel structure. Additionally, word groups formed of adjectives plus nouns are common in parallel structure.

Examples   The snake slithered **across the road**, **into the grass**, and **toward the pond**. *(adverb phrases)*

Managing employees, **taking orders**, and **balancing the books** exhausted Tom. *(gerund phrases)*

The tyrant was **loved by few** and **hated by many** but **obeyed by all**. *(participial phrases)*

To know me is **to love me**. *(infinitive phrases)*

Soft breezes, **cool water**, and **deep shade** make a perfect vacation. *(adjective-noun word groups)*

To locate nonparallel structure in series of phrases or in phrases set together for emphasis, follow these steps:

1. Identify the phrases in the series or the phrases set up for emphasis.
2. Identify each type of phrase used.
3. If the phrases are not all the same type and structure, you have pinpointed nonparallel structure. If the phrases are *all* the same type and structure, you have identified parallel structure.

Not parallel   I want you to rake the yard, to bag the leaves, and sweeping the walk. *(two infinitive phrase and a participial phrase)*

Parallel   I want you **to rake the yard**, **to bag the leaves**, and **to sweep the walk**. *(three infinitive phrases)*

Parallel   Your jobs are **raking the yard, bagging the leaves**, and **sweeping the walk**. *(three participial phrases)*

To correct nonparallel structure, choose one type of phrase and use this form for all phrases in the series.

Not parallel   Disappointed in love, friendship that betrayed him, and cheated in business, Thomas became disillusioned.

The problem: The series consists of two participial phrases and a noun modified by a clause.

The solution: Revise the noun-clause structure to form a participial phrase. As a result, the series will consist of three participial phrases.

Parallel   **Disappointed in love, betrayed by friendship, and cheated in business,** Thomas became disillusioned.

Not parallel   Pirate Jack searched for treasure on high seas, wealthy port cities, and islands in the tropics.

The problem: The series consists of an adverb phrase, an adjective-noun word group, and a noun-adverb phrase word group.

The solution: Rewrite each item in the series as an adverb phrase, thus creating a series of adverb phrases.

Parallel   Pirate Jack searched for treasure **on high seas, in wealthy port cities,** and **on tropical islands**.

Not parallel   Travel posters, drawings I made, photographs, and colorful banners decorate the walls of my room.

The problem: Two items in the series are adjective-noun word groups, one item is a noun-clause word group, and one item is a noun.

The solution: Revise the series to consist of four adjective-noun word groups.

Parallel   **Travel posters, original drawings, unusual photographs,** and **colorful banners** decorate the walls of my room.

Identify Parallel and Nonparallel Structure in Phrases

In each sentence, underline the phrases. Above the phrases, write *parallel* or *nonparallel.*

Examples   Junior is not willing <u>to offer an apology</u>, <u>to change his ways</u>, or even <u>to admit wrongdoing</u>.
          parallel

          nonparallel
<u>Skunk spray</u>, <u>lashed by poison ivy</u>, and <u>bitten by mosquitoes</u>, Sean was not enjoying the hike.

1. Selling tickets, making popcorn, and mopping floors are all in Polly's job description.

2. To love, to dream, laughter—these are my wishes for your life.

3. Rene is characterized by fierce determination, loyalty, originality that is refreshing, and surprising sensitivity.

4. Good grief! The cat's hairs have gotten on my black pants, in my iced tea, and even in my mouth!

5. Fried in grease, wrapped in foil, then warming under lamps, the fast food was ready for a customer.

6. When I graduate from high school, I want to go to college, to buy my own house, to become a teacher, and to marry a great person.

7. Please help me get rid of the ants in the sink, counters too, and along the baseboards.

8. Sniffles that sounded wet, coughing loudly, and trembling feverishly, Freddie collapsed into bed.

9. My family saves money by clipping coupons, we shop sales, and to live frugally.

10. Frequently, clothing in thrift stores, at garage sales, and in resale shops has the most potential for creating an original look.

Revise Sentence to Correct Nonparallel Structure in Phrases

For each sentence, choose the best correction for the underlined part. If the sentence is correct as it is, choose NO CHANGE.

Example   Collecting matchbooks, <u>scrapbooks</u>, and designing jewelry are my hobbies.

    A. NO CHANGE

    B. to make scrapbooks

    C. memorable scrapbooks

    D. making scrapbooks

11. <u>Mood swings that come out of nowhere</u>, rapid physical growth, and a confused sense of identity are hallmarks of the teen years.

    A. NO CHANGE

    B. Moods

    C. Unexpected mood swings

    D. Moods that swing

12. Studies suggest that pets help people to laugh, to relax, and <u>to love</u>.

    A. NO CHANGE

    B. loving

    C. loved

    D. love them

13. Wrapped in yellow paper, <u>ribbon</u>, and topped by a bow, the gift had my undivided attention.

    A. NO CHANGE

    B. a white ribbon

    C. tying with ribbon

    D. tied with ribbon

14. I saw my mother—tapping her toe and <u>looked at her watch</u>—at the curb.

    A. NO CHANGE

    B. looking at her watch

    C. to look at her watch

    D. look at her watch

15. In Fritz's hospital room, flower arrangements sat along the windowsill, on the nightstand, and <u>the television</u>.

    A. NO CHANGE

    B. next to the television

    C. the small television

    D. the television on the dresser

16. Juggling several balls, telling silly jokes, and <u>to make balloon animals</u> are all part of a party clown's job.

    A. NO CHANGE

    B. make balloon animals

    C. making balloon animals

    D. balloon animals

17. <u>Written by a talented author</u>, published by a quality press, and sold at major bookstores, the novel was sure to be a success.

    A. NO CHANGE

    B. By a talented author

    C. Writing by a talented author

    D. A talented author writing

18. At the amusement park, I wanted to ride the roller coaster, <u>trying out the paddleboats</u>, and to find the carousel.

    A. NO CHANGE

    B. paddling the boats

    C. paddle the boats

    D. to try out the paddleboats

19. <u>Walking down the hill</u>, around the curve, and toward the lake we went.

   A. NO CHANGE

   B. To walk down the hill

   C. Down the hill

   D. Walked down the hill

20. Warren informed me, "The flea market is a place to find unusual items, <u>shopping on a budget</u>, and to sell unwanted possessions."

   A. NO CHANGE

   B. to shop on a budget

   C. shopped on a budget

   D. budget shopping

Parallel Clauses

Just as words and phrases can be used to form parallel structure, so can clauses. Parallel clauses may be used to form a series or to emphasize key ideas.

Examples   **Gina sang, Paul danced,** and **I watched.** *(main clauses in a series)*

Mom is pleased **that you did the homework, that you studied,** and **that you passed** the test. *(subordinate clauses in a series)*

What you see is **what you get.** *(clauses balanced for emphasis)*

Hardwood trees, **which lose their leaves in the fall,** differ from softwood trees, **which are evergreen.** *(clauses balanced for emphasis)*

Clauses used in parallel structure should be the same type—all main clauses or all subordinate clauses.

Not parallel Claude talked nonstop, Velma giggled constantly, and who were annoying. *(two main clauses and one subordinate clause)*

Parallel   **Claude talked nonstop, Velma giggled constantly,** and **both were annoying.** *(three main clauses)*

Not parallel Campers who have dogs, they drive motorcycles, or who need electrical outlets should use Area B. *(two subordinate clauses and one main clause)*

Parallel	Campers **who have dogs**, **who drive motorcycles**, or **who need electrical outlets** should use Area B. *(three subordinate clauses)*

To locate nonparallel structure in a series of clauses or in clauses balanced for emphasis, follow these steps:

1. Identify the items in the series or the items set up for emphasis.
2. Ask yourself two questions:

   Is each item a clause?

   Are all items the same type of clause—all main clauses or all subordinate clauses?

3. If the answer to either question is no, you have pinpointed non-parallel structure. If the answer to *both* questions is yes, you have identified parallel structure in clauses.

To correct nonparallel structure, choose one type of clause and use this form for all clauses in the series.

Not parallel	The horns that honked, the sirens that wailed, and roaring motors kept the traveler awake.

The problem: The series contains two subordinate clauses and a participial phrase.

The solution: Revise the sentence to include three subordinate clauses.

Parallel	The horns **that honked**, the sirens **that wailed**, and the motors **that roared** kept the traveler awake.

Not parallel	In my family Rick plays the violin, I play the flute, and Sonya, who is a piano player.

The problem: The series contains two main clauses and a subordinate clause.

The solution: Rewrite the subordinate clause as a main clause.

Parallel	In my family **Rick plays the violin**, **I play the flute**, and **Sonya plays the piano**.

Identify Parallel and Nonparallel Structure in Clauses

In each sentence, underline the clauses in a series or clauses set up for emphasis. If the structure is parallel, write *parallel* above the clauses. If the structure is not parallel, write *nonparallel* above the clause that is nonparallel.

Examples   Maryanne wondered <u>who had left the gift</u>, <u>who had been
                                     parallel

                <u>so thoughtful</u>.

Before <u>Dean painted the walls</u>, <u>Ellie laid the tile</u>, and

nonparallel

<u>Trudy, who added new light fixtures</u>, the room was dank

and dim.

1. It surprised Ms. Meacham that Earl made an A, that Ginger made a C, and Andy's failing grade.

2. Curious George looked under the hat, he looked under the bush, and under the chair.

3. The ones who did the work are the ones deserving the praise.

4. Julia will collect tickets, Carly, who will pass out programs, and Oliver will seat people.

5. When I say I'm sorry, I mean I'm sorry.

6. The river, which runs past my farm and irrigating my fields, teems with fish.

7. The recipe calls for butter that is soft and that is unsalted—no exceptions.

8. Residents whose homes were flooded, businesses damaged, or whose families were injured should contact the disaster relief team.

9. A critic of the movie declared, "It will amuse you, it will shock you, which will change you."

10. Home is where your heart is, where you hang your hat, or where your roots go deep.

Revise Sentences to Create Parallel Structure in Clauses

Rewrite all or part of each sentence to correct nonparallel structure in clauses. If the sentence is best unchanged, write *no change*.

Examples   Mercury orbits closest to the sun, Venus orbits next closest, and Earth being third closest.

Earth orbits third closest.

The music that you like and the music that I like are two entirely different styles.

<u>*no change*</u>

11. The streets that are cracked, that have potholes, or crumbling are first in priority for repairs.

12. Grandmother wondered if Brad made the football team, Sammie who found a job, and if Ashley entered the art contest.

13. Dusk fell, streetlights blinked on, and families gathered for dinner.

14. Birds twittered, bees droned, dogs that barked, and children who played.

15. When I give you the signal is when you drop the curtain.

16. The baby squalled during Act One, it squalled during intermission, and during Act Five.

17. David keeps breath mints in his locker, keeping them in his car, and he keeps them in his book bag.

18. Villagers raised corn, who herded cattle, or who cultivated fruit trees met to discuss the drought.

19. I came, I saw, I conquered.

20. The science project that Brenda designed and built by Gage won first place.

Multiple Choice
Choose the best revision for each underlined part. If the part is best left unchanged, choose NO CHANGE.

Vermeer: Painter of Quiet Beauty

The 1600s in Europe were known as the Golden Age

of Art, thanks to the paintings of Rembrandt van Rijn,

Pieter de Hooch, <u>an artist named Jan Steen</u>, and other
                      1

artists. In Holland, Johannes Vermeer, born in 1632 and

_____ **1. A.** NO CHANGE
     B. Jan Steen
     C. an artists whose name is Jan Steen
     D. Jan Steen, an artist

<u>he was raised in his father's inn</u>, became a respected
         2

painter in Delft.

Vermeer is known for creating scenes of quietness,

_____ **2. A.** NO CHANGE
     B. to be raised in his father's inn
     C. raising in his father's inn
     D. raised in his father's inn

<u>a sense of being still</u>, and beauty. His settings are typi-
     3

_____ **3. A.** NO CHANGE
     B. being still
     C. stillness
     D. of being still

cally indoor, <u>his subjects are usually men and women</u>,
                      4

and his palette is generally muted and soft. Many works

feature subjects who are lost in thought, busy at a task,

_____ **4. A.** NO CHANGE
     B. usually men and women
     C. his subjects men and women
     D. usually, men and women are his subjects

or <u>they are arranged in intimate groupings</u>. In many
          5

paintings, light from a window washes the scene in a

soft glow. To enliven the soft golds, muted greens, and

_____ **5. A.** NO CHANGE
     B. arranging in intimate groupings
     C. arranged in intimate groupings
     D. to arrange in intimate groupings

warm browns of the color palette, Vermeer often included
6

small touches of vivid red. A pattern on a tablecloth, a bit

_____ 6. **6. A.** NO CHANGE
B. brown
C. warms
D. warm shades of brown

of lace, or a curtain that he painted hanging at a
7

window shimmers with reddish hues.
7

　　When Vermeer was twenty years old, his father died.

7. A. NO CHANGE
B. a curtain to hang at a window
C. a painted curtain
D. a curtain at a window

Afterward Vermeer ran the family inn, sold artworks
8

and silk cloth, and married Catharina Bolnes. The

couple's family grew over the years to include fifteen

children. Somehow Vermeer found time to raise a

8. A. NO CHANGE
B. to run the family inn
C. running of the family inn
D. the family inn

family, to run the inn, and creating beautiful paintings.
9

However, after his death in 1675, his paintings were

9. A. NO CHANGE
B. to create beautiful paintings
C. creator of beautiful paintings
D. beautiful paintings that he created

scattered, his name it was forgotten. Not until the
10

late 1800s did Vermeer's name and artworks regain

a place of recognition and honor in the world

of art.

10. A. NO CHANGE
B. his forgotten name
C. forgetting his name
D. his name was forgotten

Short Answer

Use the checklist to answer the following question.

Writer's Checklist

✓ Phrases
✓ Modifiers
✓ Parallel Structure

Outraged by the verdict, the reporters were told that the defense would file an appeal, winning the appeal, and vindicate their client.

You have been asked by a fellow student to peer edit the above sentence. Using the checklist, give the writer feedback by identifying the two rules to apply in order to improve the sentence. Then rewrite the sentence correctly.

Lesson 3 OGT Practice: Grammar

Multiple Choice

Instructions: Certain words and phrases in the following passage are underlined and numbered. In the right-hand column, you will find alternatives for each underlined part. Choose the revision that best conforms to the rules of grammar. If the original version is best, choose NO CHANGE.

Sanity in Space

When a crew of astronauts rockets off into space,

many factors determine their well-being. The spacecraft

must be in top-notch repair, <u>the crew being</u> precisely
1

trained, and each astronaut's mental stability must be

reliable.

    1. **A.** NO CHANGE
        B. the crew to be
        C. the crew must be
        D. the crew, which is

Think about it. When was the last time you took a

lengthy car trip <u>of people with a group</u>? How long was
2

it until someone <u>get</u> on someone else's nerves? Now
3

think about this. What if you were in the far reaches of

    2. **A.** NO CHANGE
        B. with a group of people
        C. with people of a group
        D. of people a group

    3. **A.** NO CHANGE
        B. getting
        C. got
        D. getted

<u>space. Packed</u> in a spacecraft with a group of other
4

people? How long do you think it would take for

    4. **A.** NO CHANGE
        B. space that is
        C. space; packed
        D. space, packed

tempers <u>to flare</u> or for personalities to clash?
5

    One of the ways astronauts keep their mental cool is

by bringing along a small reminder of home—a family

photograph, for example. Astronaut Charles Duke

    5. **A.** NO CHANGE
        B. flaring
        C. flared
        D. being flared up

will take a family photo with him on his trip to the
6

moon in 1972.

Another method of maintain peace and harmony
7

is sending up a "mixed bag" of astronauts: an introvert,

an extrovert, a take-charge person, a person who
8

is a peacekeeper, a nurturing type, and so on.
8

Thus combined, each person is able to do what he or
9

she does best in mini-turf wars without clashing.
10

6. **A.** NO CHANGE
   B. took
   C. had took
   D. had taken

7. **A.** NO CHANGE
   B. of maintaining peace and harmony
   C. of which is maintaining peace and harmony
   D. of maintain peace and harmony

8. **A.** NO CHANGE
   B. peacekeeper
   C. a peacekeeper
   D. peacekeeping

9. **A.** NO CHANGE
   B. Thus to combine
   C. Thus combine
   D. Thus that is combined

10. **A.** NO CHANGE
    B. clashing in mini-turf wars
    C. in mini-turf wars
    D. without clashing in mini-turf wars

Short Answer

Use the checklist to answer the following question.

Writer's Checklist

✓ Verb Tense

✓ Phrases

✓ Main and Subordinate Clauses

✓ Parallel Structure

Going to the zoo was a great experience because in one place you can see giraffes nibbling from trees, walruses that swim in the pool, lions lounge in the shade, and gazelles grazing in the field.

You have been asked by a fellow student to peer edit the above. Using the checklist, give the writer feedback by identifying the two rules that apply to the errors in the sentence. Then rewrite the sentence correctly.

_____

_____

_____

_____

_____

_____

_____

_____

_____

PART FOUR | Practice Tests

OGT WRITING

Practice Test 1

PART ONE: RESPONDING TO WRITING PROMPTS

Directions: Write a complete, edited response to *each* of the following two writing topics. You may start with either topic. You will have 2½ hours to complete the entire test, including the multiple-choice portion that follows. Pace yourself accordingly.

Use the blank pages for prewriting. Your prewriting is an important part of the writing process and should be completed. However, your prewriting will not be scored. The **drafts** you want **scored** should be written on the lined pages. These drafts need to be legible; they may be in printed or in cursive handwriting.

Revise and edit your writing. Erasing, crossing out, and other editing changes may be made right on the drafts themselves.

Go on to the next page.

TOPIC FOR WRITING #1

Your school newspaper is holding a contest for the best story about a disagreement between friends. The winning story will be printed for the enjoyment of high school readers. For the contest, write a narrative depicting a disagreement between friends. Tell what the disagreement was about and where the conflict took place. Develop your story with details.

Go on to the next page.

PREWRITING: Nothing on this page will be scored.

Go on to the next page.

_____

_____

_____

_____

_____

_____

_____

_____

_____

_____

_____

_____

_____

_____

_____

_____

_____

_____

_____

_____

_____

Go on to the next page.

Go on to the next page.

TOPIC FOR WRITING, #2

Your mayor is considering a teen curfew of 9:00 P.M. on week-nights because of a problem with vandalism. Write a letter to the editor of your local newspaper in which you convince readers to accept your point of view on the proposed curfew. Be specific in developing your argument.

Go on to the next page.

PREWRITING: Nothing on this page will be scored.

Go on to the next page.

Go on to the next page.

Go on to the next page.

PART TWO: RESPONDING TO MULTIPLE-CHOICE QUESTIONS

Instructions: Certain words and phrases in the following passage are underlined and numbered. In the right-hand column, you will find alternatives for each underlined part. Choose the alternative showing the best way to revise and improve the selection. If the original version is best, choose NO CHANGE.

Teen Court in Ohio

According to the National Youth Court Center,

eleven teen <u>courts are</u> located across Ohio. Other teen
1

     1. A. NO CHANGE
          B. court's are
          C. courts, are
          D. court's, are

courts not listed with this <u>organizeation</u> also practice in
2

     2. A. NO CHANGE
          B. organzation
          C. organizateton
          D. organization

various Ohio cities. These legal courts <u>exist</u> for one
3

     3. A. NO CHANGE
          B. existed
          C. existing
          D. will exist

reason: to help young people. To do so, they enlist the

aid of judges and lawyers as well as teenage volunteers

from the community.

The teen court is presided over by a <u>judge. Who</u> is
4

     4. A. NO CHANGE
          B. judge who
          C. judge, who
          D. judge; who

typically a judge or lawyer volunteering for the duty.

The jury is formed of teenagers—often high schoolers—

who are specially trained. Together, the judge and jury

work to help the defendant <u>the offender</u>.
5

     5. A. NO CHANGE
          B. being the offender
          C. the Offender
          D. (the offender)

The defendant is typically between the ages of ten

and seventeen and is a first-time offender. The

Go on to the next page.

defendant who pleads guilty to the charge, <u>accepting</u>
₆

the sentence of the jury, and completes the teen court

process is rewarded. All formal charges are dropped.

During the court session, jury members <u>questioned</u>
₇

the defendant about the offense. They may ask about

the defendant's feelings and opinions and about the

effects <u>on family members of the actions</u>. They may also
₈

question the defendant's parents or guardians. Then,

with the judge's help, the jury uses this information to

devise a sentence.

If the defendant completes the sentence by the due

<u>date. Juvenile</u> Court drops the formal charges. The
₉

defendant has a chance to make a new start, <u>keeps</u> his
₁₀

or her legal record clean.

_____ 6. **A.** NO CHANGE
     B. to accept
     C. accepts
     D. accepted

_____ 7. **A.** NO CHANGE
     B. question
     C. questioning
     D. to question

_____ 8. **A.** NO CHANGE
     B. of the actions on family members
     C. about family members of the actions
     D. of the actions about family members

_____ 9. **A.** NO CHANGE
     B. date juvenile
     C. date: Juvenile
     D. date, Juvenile

_____ 10. **A.** NO CHANGE
     B. kept
     C. to keep
     D. keep

Go on to the next page.

PART THREE: RESPONDING TO SHORT-ANSWER QUESTIONS

Use the checklist to answer the following question.

Writer's Checklist

Good writing includes the following:

✓ Standard English
✓ Correct Sentence Structure
✓ Verb Tense and Agreement
✓ Parallel Structure

Born in Mississippi in 1927. Leontyne Price grows up to become a great American opera singer.

You have been asked by a fellow student to peer edit the above sentences. Using the checklist, give the writer feedback by identifying the two rules that apply to the errors in the sentences. Then rewrite them correctly.

_____

_____

_____

_____

_____

_____

_____

_____

STOP.

OGT WRITING

Practice Test 2

PART ONE: RESPONDING TO WRITING TOPICS

Directions: Write a complete, edited response to each of the following two writing topics. You may start with either topic; divide your time as you think appropriate.

Use the blank pages for prewriting. Your prewriting is an important part of the writing process and should be completed. However, your prewriting will not be scored. The **drafts** you want **scored** should be written on the lined pages. These drafts need to be legible; they may be in printed or in cursive handwriting.

Revise and edit your writing. Erasing, crossing out, and other editing changes may be made right on the drafts themselves.

Go on to the next page.

TOPIC FOR WRITING #1

Your school's principal is considering offering a driver's education course free of charge to sophomores each year. Taken at other locations, the same course would cost $225. Opponents of the proposal say that school time is for taking classes in traditional subjects, not for "giving students a free ride" in driver's ed. What do you think? Write a letter to your principal, persuading him or her to see your point of view. Use appropriate facts, opinions, and details to support your ideas.

Go on to the next page.

PREWRITING: Nothing on this page will be scored.

Go on to the next page.

_____

_____

_____

_____

_____

_____

_____

_____

_____

_____

_____

_____

_____

_____

_____

_____

_____

_____

_____

_____

_____

_____

_____

Go on to the next page.

Go on to the next page.

TOPIC FOR WRITING #2

A kid's day camp in your community needs volunteers this summer. To qualify, an individual must be at least thirteen years of age, have a reliable method of getting to the day camp each day, and have an enthusiastic, fun attitude. Areas needing volunteers are sports, crafts, music, and quiet time. Write an essay explaining your desire and ability to volunteer in one of these areas. Include relevant facts and details.

Go on to the next page.

PREWRITING: Nothing on this page will be scored.

Go on to the next page.

_____

_____

_____

_____

_____

_____

_____

_____

_____

_____

_____

_____

_____

_____

_____

_____

_____

_____

_____

_____

_____

_____

Go on to the next page.

Go on to the next page.

Instructions: Certain words and phrases in the following passage are underlined and numbered. In the right-hand column, you will find alternatives for each underlined part. Choose the alternative showing the best way to revise and improve the selection. If the original version is best, choose NO CHANGE.

The Object of My Affection

We've all done it. Just admit <u>it, at</u> one time or
₁
another, we have all gone to great lengths to attract

the object of our affection, whether that person be

male or female. We scrutinize <u>our hair; our face; our</u>
₂
<u>shape</u> in the mirror. We stare blankly into the closet,
₂
wondering what to wear to make ourselves

noticeable in a casual, I-just-threw-this-on kind

of way.

Perhaps (while alone) we practice speaking to our

<u>desired one, judging</u> the timbre of our voice. Do I
₃

sound squeaky? one might ask. Do I sound confident,

<u>inviting</u>, alluring? If I call him (or her) up on the
₄

_____ 1. **A.** NO CHANGE
   B. it; At
   C. it at
   D. it! At

_____ 2. **A.** NO CHANGE
   B. our hair, our face, and our shape
   C. our hair, face, and our shape
   D. our hair; face, and our shape

_____ 3. **A.** NO CHANGE
   B. desired one. Judging
   C. desired one: judging
   D. desired one and judge

_____ 4. **A.** NO CHANGE
   B. invite
   C. to invited
   D. am inviting

Go on to the next page.

telephone, can I <u>simply say, hi, it's me, and</u> he'll know
5

my voice?

Who among us hasn't dabbed on just a little too

much cologne? Who <u>hasn't weeped</u> over a hair disaster
6

or swiveled around to check the appearance of one's

behind in the <u>mirror. More</u> important, who hasn't popped
7

a mint before a significant encounter, hoping the onions

from the Salisbury steak at lunch won't speak louder than

our words?

    Indeed, all of us fall prey to the urge to spruce up

a bit, <u>to have put our best foot forward</u>, to present
8

ourselves in our best light. We market ourselves. We sell

ourselves with our appearance and words. We fear our

best <u>sell points</u> are obscured by our insecurities.
9

    But perhaps they are not so obscured. Chances are,

the object of our affection <u>knew</u> a little bit about self-
10

scrutiny too.

---

5. A. NO CHANGE
  B. simply say, "Hi, it's me," and
  C. simply say hi, it's me and
  D. simply say, "Hi, its me," and

6. A. NO CHANGE
  B. has'nt weeped
  C. hasn't wept
  D. has not weeped

7. A. NO CHANGE
  B. mirror! More
  C. mirror? More
  D. mirror: more

8. A. NO CHANGE
  B. to put our best foot forward
  C. to be putting our best foot forward
  D. put our best foot forward

9. A. NO CHANGE
  B. to sell points
  C. sold points
  D. selling points

10. A. NO CHANGE
  B. new
  C. knows
  D. known

Go on to the next page.

PART THREE: RESPONDING TO SHORT-ANSWER QUESTIONS

Use the checklist to answer the following question.

Writer's Checklist

Good writing includes the following:

✓ Standard English
✓ Verb Tense and Agreement
✓ Punctuation
✓ Complete Sentences

After the Titanic had sank, new regulations were enacted to govern sea travel especially travel near ice fields.

You have been asked by a fellow student to peer edit the above. Using the checklist, give the writer feedback by identifying the two rules that apply to the errors in the sentence. Then rewrite the sentence correctly.

STOP.

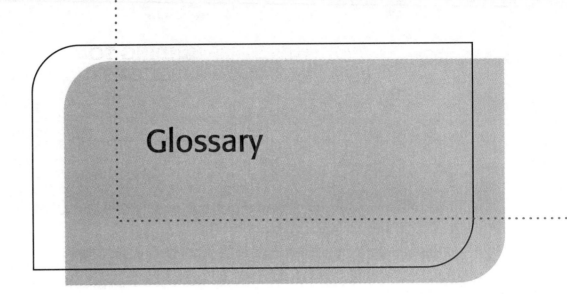

Glossary

academic content standard   A statement of learning goals in a particular subject in school. The Ohio Graduation Test in Writing covers learning goals in English Language Arts—specifically, the Writing Processes standard, the Writing Applications standard, and the Writing Conventions standard.

adjective   Part of speech that modifies a noun or a pronoun.

adjective clause   A subordinate clause that modifies a noun or a pronoun.

adjective phrase   A phrase that modifies a noun or a pronoun.

adverb   Part of speech that modifies a verb, an adjective, or another adverb.

adverb clause   A subordinate clause that modifies a verb, an adjective, or an adverb.

adverb phrase   A phrase used to modify a verb, an adjective, or an adverb.

benchmark   A specific skill necessary to mastering an academic content standard. The Ohio Graduation Test in Writing is based upon the benchmarks for the Writing Processes standard, the Writing Applications standard, and the Writing Conventions standard.

body   The paragraphs of a paper or essay that develop and prove the thesis, or main idea. The body follows the introduction and comes before the conclusion. In a business letter, the body is made up of all the paragraphs of the letter. It follows the salutation (such as "Dear Mr. Smith:") and comes before the closing (such as "Sincerely, James Jones").

brainstorming   A prewriting technique used to develop or clarify ideas and information. A writer jots down all ideas—expressed in words, phrases, or sentences—that come to mind in relation to a particular topic.

character   A person (or sometimes a creature) in a narrative, made real through sensory details (sight, feel, taste, touch, smell) and concrete language (specific details).

clause   A word group that contains both a subject and its verb. A clause may be a main clause (it can stand alone as a sentence) or a subordinate clause (it cannot stand alone).

coherence   A quality of good writing. Coherent writing has a clear, logical structure; flows logically from one idea or detail to the next; and uses transitions to show relationships between ideas.

conclusion   The final paragraph(s) of a paper, which tie together the paper's main ideas and give closure to the paper.

conflict   The problem or tension in a narrative that determines the structure of the plot.

conjunction   Part of speech that links words, phrases, clauses, or sentences.

conventions   Rules for spelling, punctuation, capitalization, and grammar.

dangling modifier   A modifier that does not clearly and logically modify a word in the sentence.

declarative sentence   A statement of a fact or other information. A declarative sentence ends with a period.

dialogue   Written conversation in a narrative.

editing   The stage in the writing process during which the writer corrects errors in content, organization, and conventions in order to create a polished draft.

exclamatory sentence   A statement showing strong emotion. An exclamatory sentence ends with an exclamation point (!).

expository writing   Writing whose goal is to explain, to make information clear. It may draw briefly on persuasion, description, or narration to help achieve its purpose.

focus   A quality of good writing. Focused writing centers on one main idea; each paragraph supports that main idea.

foreshadowing   A literary technique of giving hints or clues to events that will happen later in the narrative.

gerund   A verbal (verb form) ending in *-ing* that is used as a noun in a sentence.

gerund phrase   A phrase made up of a gerund and its modifiers and/or complements. A gerund phrase is used as a noun in a sentence.

graphic organizer   A method of organizing ideas and information using diagrams and other pictorial methods. An example is the cluster diagram.

homophones   Two (or more) words that have the same pronunciation but different spellings and meanings. Examples are *your, you're,* and *to, too, two.*

imperative sentence   A statement of a command or request. An imperative sentence ends with a period or an exclamation point.

infinitive   A verbal (verb form) usually formed of *to* plus the present tense of a verb. An infinitive is used as a noun, an adjective, or an adverb in a sentence.

infinitive phrase   A phrase made up of an infinitive and its modifiers, complements, and/or objects. An infinitive phrase is used as a noun, an adjective, or an adverb in a sentence.

interjection   The part of speech used to express a simple exclamation (such as *Hey!* or *Wow!*). When an interjection is used to begin a sentence, it is set off by a comma, as in *Yes, I know that.*

interrogative sentence   The expression of a question. An interrogative sentence ends with a question mark (?).

introduction   The part of a passage that presents the central idea and thesis.

irregular verb   A verb whose past and past participle are formed in some way other than by adding *-d* or *-ed* to the present form. Examples are *break, broke, have broken* and *swim, swam, have swum.*

main clause   A word group that contains both a subject and its verb. It may stand alone as a sentence, or it may be linked to another main clause or subordinate clause to form a sentence.

main idea   The controlling idea or concept of a paper, report, letter, or other written text. All paragraphs in the text explain, develop, or support the main idea.

mechanics   The form of words, including capitalization and spelling, and the punctuation of words and sentences.

misplaced modifier   A modifier that is not placed next to the word or word group it modifies, causing the reader to misunderstand the sentence.

modifier   A word or word group that makes the meaning of another word or word group more specific and clear. Adjectives and adverbs are modifiers.

narrative writing   A text that relates a series of events (real or imaginary), either to provide entertainment or to reveal a moral or lesson.

noun   Part of speech that names a person, place, thing, or idea.

outline   A plan for the structure of a piece of writing. Formal outlines use roman numerals, capital letters, and sometimes numbers to show the structure of main and supporting ideas. An informal outline may use a bulleted list or another method of grouping ideas and planning structure.

paragraph   A group of related sentences, often made up of a main (or topic) sentence and supporting sentences.

parallel structure   The use of the same grammatical form to list items in a series or to balance ideas for emphasis.

participle   A verb form that is used as part of a verb phrase or as an adjective. The present participle of a verb ends in *-ing*. The past participle of a regular verb is formed by adding *-ed* to the present form. The past participle of an irregular verb is formed in some other way.

participial phrase   A phrase made up of a participle and any objects, complements, and modifiers. It is used as an adjective in a sentence.

phrase   A group of related words used as a single part of speech in a sentence. A phrase does not contain both a subject and its verb, and it cannot stand alone as a sentence.

plot   The events of a narrative, usually centered on one or more conflicts. Plot structure is formed of conflict, rising action, climax, and resolution to the conflict. The plot may use literary devices such as foreshadowing and flashback.

point of view   The perspective from which a narrative is told, such as third-person point of view *(he, she, they)* or first-person point of view (*I, us, we*).

prefix   A letter or group of letters added to the beginning of a word root or base word to change the meaning of the word, as *un-* in *unpack*.

preposition   Part of speech that shows the relationship between its object(s) and another word in the sentence.

prepositional phrase   A word group made up of a preposition, its object, and any modifiers of the object. The object of a preposition is a noun or pronoun, and the object may be compound (more than one noun or pronoun).

prewriting   The stage of the writing process during which the writer determines the purpose for writing, identifies the audience, jots down ideas, and plans a method of organization.

pronoun   Part of speech that takes the place of a noun and is used in sentences just as nouns are used.

punctuation   Use of periods, commas, apostrophes, colons, and other marks to make the meanings of written words and sentences specific and clear.

regular verb   A verb whose past and past participle are formed by adding *-d* or *-ed* to the present form. Examples are *walk, walked* and *paste, pasted*.

revision   The stage of the writing process during which the writer makes changes to improve the presentation of ideas, the structure, individual sentences, or other aspects of the draft.

sentence   A word group containing a subject and a predicate. Sentences are classified by purpose (declarative, imperative, interrogative, exclamatory), and by structure (simple, compound, complex, compound-complex).

setting   The time and place of the events and actions of a narrative.

standard   See *academic content standard*.

subordinate clause   A word group that does not contain both a subject and its verb. A subordinate clause cannot stand alone and must be linked with one or more main clauses to form a sentence.

suffix   A letter or group of letters added to the end of a word root or base word to change the meaning or function of the word, as *-ly* in *friendly*.

transition   A word, phrase, or sentence that helps move the reader's attention smoothly from one idea to the next. Transitions help explain the relationships between ideas.

tense   The form of a verb that indicates time. English has six basic verb tenses: present, past, future, present perfect, past perfect, and future perfect.

thesis   A statement of the central point or main argument of a piece of writing.

topic   The specific, central idea of a piece of writing, often stated in a word or phrase.

topic sentence   A statement of the central idea of a paragraph or passage.

verb   Part of speech that expresses action or links the subject to another word in the sentence.

verbal   A verb form used as a noun, an adjective, or an adverb in a sentence. The three types of verbals are gerunds, participles, and infinitives.

verbal phrase   A verbal and any objects, complements, and/or modifiers. Gerund phrases, participial phrases, and infinitive phrases are types of verbal phrases.

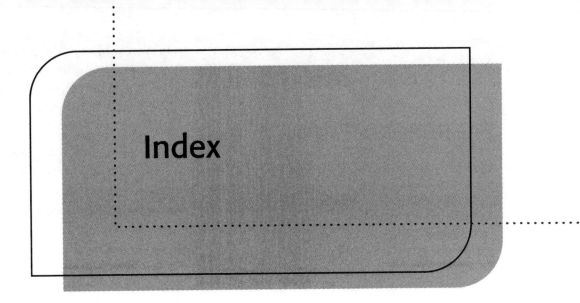

Index